D0170213

Dictionary of
1000 Spanish Proverbs
With English Equivalents

Dictionary of
1000 Spanish Proverbs

With English Equivalents

Peter Mertvago

HIPPOCRENE BOOKS
New York

Copyright© 1996 by Hippocrene Books, Inc.

All rights reserved.

For information, address:
HIPPOCRENE BOOKS, INC.
171 Madison Avenue
New York, NY 10016

Cataloging-in-Publication Data

Mertvago, Peter.
        Dictionary of 1000 Spanish proverbs : with English equivalents / Pete
Mertvago.
        p.   cm.
        Includes bibliographical references.
        ISBN 0-7818-0412-4
        1. Proverbs, Spanish. 2. Proverbs, Spanish—Translations into English
I. Title.
PN6491.M47   1996   95-51082
398.9'61—dc20   CIP

Printed in the United States of America.

To Pica
for the idea of this book

Introduction

Proverbs and Language

Proverbs have been variously described as succinct and often didactic statements embodying the traditional wisdom of a people or as moral metaphors based on natural observation tersely summarizing experience. The immortal Cervantes, to whose credit is perhaps the greatest literary use of what in Spanish had hitherto been an oral form of popular expression, characterized proverbs as short sentences based on long experience.

From a linguistic point of view, if languages are considered to be semiotic systems which communicate information by means of *signs* or *semeia* that stand for specific ideas, objects or situations in the real world, proverbs function as complex units which dispense a speaker from the need of any prior formulation of concepts that are already current in a ready-made form in his or her cultural group. This is borne out by the Latin etymology of the word given by the OED: *pro* + *verbum* (word) + *ium* (collective suffix) hence meaning "a (recognized) set of words put forth." In Spanish, the word *refrán* has been used synonymously and interchangeably with the word *proverbio* since the XVth century and this, much as in the English expression *"the old refrain,"* further underscores the frequent and repetitive use of proverbs in the spoken idiom.

Consequently, for a student of Spanish or anyone else wishing to communicate effectively in the language, the most common proverbs have to be understood and learnt in the same way that idioms and individual words must be mastered.

The Spanish Proverb

To the extent that there is a uniform pool of human experience and interborrowing from common historical and cultural antecedents, the Spanish proverb is largely a Spanish counterpart of similar expressions that are intrinsic to European and even universal folk-lore.

Roman, Christian and Arabic influences have been pointed out in the apparently profound philosophical and religious content and rendering of many Spanish proverbs and sayings, which in other languages exist in a less austere form. Thus we have expressions like *a los bobos aparece la madre de Dios* and *abad avariento por un bodigo pierde ciento* for what in English is said simply by *fortune (luck) is wasted on fools* and *penny wise and pound foolish*. Such a religious leaning may also have been prompted by the fact that the oldest collections of Spanish proverbs were compiled by monks in the Middle Ages and were used ostensibly in the moral education of youth.

The antiquity of Spanish proverbs can be seen in their emergence as early as the fourteenth and fifteenth centuries. Though their use was frowned upon by the aristocracy as something more denotative of the vulgar masses, no less a nobleman than the erudite Marqués de Santillana compiled his celebrated *Proverbios que dizen las viejas tras el fuego* in the middle of the fifteenth century. This work was actually first published around the turn of that century, or shortly thereafter (1512?), some 50 years after his death, as a result of the general interest spurred all over Europe by Erasmus' *Adages*, which appeared in 1500. In Spain, de Santillana's work was followed by Pedro Vallés, who published his collection of some 4000 proverbs entitled *Libro de refranes* in Zaragoza in 1549,[1] and then by Fernán Núñez de

---

1   A limited facsimile edition of this work was published by García Moreno in 1917; only three copies of the original have survived.

Guzmán, whose collection of 6000 proverbs came out in 1555, and included many French, Italian and Portuguese proverbs. From those beginnings there unfolded four centuries of Spanish paremiography for which the interested reader may be referred to the excellent bibliography given by Richard Jente in his article about the Spanish proverb.[2]

How to Use This Book

This book is a selective collection of what in the opinion of the author makes up the 1000 most important and commonly used and understood proverbs of *Castillian* Spanish as it is spoken and written today. It is neither an exhaustive compilation nor does it include proverbs that may be current in specific overseas Spanish-speaking regions or countries, such as Latin America. This in itself is an interesting subject for comparative study but would transcend the scope of this book.

The entries have been arranged as in a dictionary, in Spanish alphabetical order by Spanish key word and numbered consecutively from 1 to 1000. For the purposes of this book, a *key word* is the sequentially first noun most closely associated with the meaning of the proverb and/or having a greater linguistic range or frequency. For proverbs without nouns, key words may be verbs, adjectives or adverbs used on the basis of the same considerations. Alternate variations of proverbs or alternate words or phrases used in the same proverb are placed within parentheses in the entry that represents the most common form of the proverb.

An important distinction is made in providing the English equivalents of the proverbs. For many Spanish proverbs there is an exact or nearly exact word-for-word equivalent in English where the same proverb exists in both languages in an identical

---

2   Jente, Richard, "El Refrán." *Folklore Americas,* VII nos. 1-2 (1947), pp. 7-10.

or easily recognizable and closely-related alternate form. In such cases, the English proverb appears below the Spanish entry in normal type. But where no lexically-equivalent proverb exists in English, rather than provide a translation of the Spanish, the book offers actual English proverbs[3] that would be used in similar contexts or circumstances. This is consistent with the treatment of proverbs as semiotic units that communicate entire thoughts in an encapsulated, ready-made format. Such equivalents are set in *italics* and it is assumed that the reader, once aware of the meaning or sense of a proverb and if so inclined, may proceed to identify the lexical differences by using standard monolingual or bilingual dictionaries if necessary. English proverbs that have a meaning opposite to that of the Spanish entry may be listed for comparison, in which case they are marked by a dagger [†]. An English Key Word Index is provided to facilitate the use of the book from English into Spanish.

---

3   For the purposes of this book, English proverbs mean either British or American proverbs. British spelling has been used throughout, with the exception of those proverbs whose provenance is recognized as being exclusively American.

Acknowledgment

The author wishes to thank Tomás de Echevarría for his invaluable assistance in preparing and proofreading the manuscript for publication.

A

Abad	1	Abad avariento, por un bodigo pierde ciento. *Penny wise and pound foolish.*
	2	Como canta el abad, responde el monacillo (sacristán). *Like priest, like people. As the old cock crows, the young cock learns.*
Abarcar	3	Quien mucho abarca, poco aprieta. *He who begins many things, finishes but few. Grasp all, lose all.*
Abril	4	Abril, aguas mil. *April showers bring May flowers.*
Abogado	5	Buen abogado, mal vecino. A good lawyer, a bad neighbour.
Aceite	6	Quien el aceite mesura, las manos se unta. He that measureth oil shall anoint his fingers. *He that deals in dirt has aye foul fingers.*
Acabar	7	Bien está lo que bien acaba. All's well that ends well.

Acometer	8	Acometer hace vencer. *He who never tries anything will never win.*
Adán	9	Todos somos hijos de Adán (y Eva). We are all Adam's children.
Adquiridor	10	A buen adquiridor, buen expendedor. *Closely gathered, widely spent.*
Adquirir	11	Los bienes mal adquiridos a nadie han enriquecido. Ill-gotten goods seldom prosper.
Afán	12	A cada día su afán. *No day passes without some grief.*
Afición	13	Afición ciega razón. Affection blinds reason.
Agraz	14	Unos comen el agraz y otros tienen la dentera. *One does the scathe and another has the scorn.*
Agua	15	Agua pasada no mueve molino. Water that's passed cannot make the mill go.
	16	Cada uno quiere llevar el agua a su molino, y dejar en seco el del vecino. *Every man drags water to his own mill.*
Aguila	17	Del águila no nace la paloma. Eagles don't breed doves.
	18	El águila no caza moscas. Eagles don't catch flies.
Agujero	19	Escucha al agujero, oirás de tu mal y del ajeno. *Listen at the keyhole and you'll hear bad news about yourself.*

Ajuste	20	Más vale mal ajuste (concierto) que buen pleito.
		A lean agreement is better than a fat judgment.

Alabar	21	Nadie se alabe hasta que acabe.
		Call no man happy till he is dead.

Alcanzar	22	Alcanza quien no se cansa.
		Achievement is one percent aspiration and ninety-nine percent perspiration. He who does not tire, tires adversity.

Alegría	23	Alegrías, antruejo, que mañana será(n) ceniza(s).
		After Christmas comes Lent.
	24	No hay alegría sin tristeza.
		No joy without annoy.

Algo	25	Más vale algo que nada.
		Something is better than nothing.

Alguacil	26	Cada uno tiene su alguacil.
		You cannot hide from your conscience.

Amar	27	Cada cual ama lo suyo.
		Every man likes his own things best.
	28	Quien feo ama, hermoso le parece.
		Love sees no faults. In the eye of the lover, pock marks are dimples. Beauty is in the eye of the beholder.

Amenazar	29	Más son los amenazados que los acuchillados (heridos).
		There are more threatened than stricken.

Amigo	30	Amigo beneficiado, enemigo declarado.
		Lend your money and lose your friend.

31 Amigo de todos y de ninguno, todo es uno.
A friend to all is a friend to none.

32 Amigo del buen tiempo, múdase con el viento.
Fair-weather friends are not worth having.

33 Amigo reconciliado, enemigo doblado.
A reconciled friend is a double enemy.

34 Aquellos son ricos, que tienen amigos.
They are rich who have true friends.

35 Cárceles y caminos hacen amigos.
In a long journey and a small inn, one knows one's company.

36 Dos amigos de una bolsa, el uno canta y el otro llora.
When two friends have a common purse, one sings and the other weeps.

37 El amigo imprudente es más dañado que el enemigo declarado.
A rash friend is worse than a foe.

38 Entre amigos y soldados, cumplimentos son excusados.
A good friend never offends.

39 Más vale(n) amigo(s) en plaza que dinero(s) en casa (arca).
A friend in the market is better than money in the chest.

40 Más vale un amigo que pariente o primo.
A good friend is my nearest relation.

41 Reniego del amigo que cubre con las alas y muerde con el pico.
He covers me with his wings and bites me with his bill.

Amo	42	De tal amo, tal criado. Like master, like man.
	43	El ojo del amo engorda el caballo. The master's eye makes the horse fat.
Amor	44	Amor de niño, agua en cesto (cestillo). *Love of lads and fire of chats is soon in and soon out.*
	45	Amores nuevos olvidan viejos. *Old love burns low when new love breaks.*
	46	Donde hay amor, hay dolor. *Love is a sweet torment.*
	47	El amor es un pasatiempo que pasa con el tiempo. Love makes time pass, time makes love pass.
Andar	48	Quien mal anda, mal acaba. *An ill life, an ill end.*
Angel	49	De joven ángel, viejo diablo. Young saint, old devil.
Anima	50	Una ánima sola, ni canta ni llora. A soul alone neither sings nor weeps.
Año	51	Al cabo de cien años, todos seremos calvos. After a hundred years, we shall all be bald.
	52	Lo que no acaece (se hace) en un año, acaece (se hace) en un rato. *It chances in an hour, that happens not in seven years.*
	53	No hay ninguno tan viejo que no piense vivir un año. None so old that he hopes not for a year of life.

Apariencia	54	Las apariencias engañan. Appearances are deceiving.
Arbol	55	Del árbol caído todos hacen leña. When the tree is fallen, everyone runs to it with an axe.
	56	El árbol por el fruto es conocido. A tree is known by its fruit.
	57	El más grande árbol fue antes arborillo. *Great oaks from little acorns grow.*
Arco	58	Arco siempre armado, o flojo o quebrado. *A bow too much bent will break.*
Arte	59	Quien tiene arte, va por toda parte. Who has a trade has a share everywhere.
Arroyo	60	Los pequeños arroyos hacen los grandes ríos. Little streams make big rivers.
Asno	61	Asno con oro, alcánzalo todo. *An ass laden with gold climbs to the top of the castle.*
	62	Asno de muchos, lobos se lo comen. *The common horse is worst shod.*
	63	Bien sabe el asno en cuya cara rebuzna. The ass knows in whose face it brays.
	64	Cuando todos te dijeren que eres asno, rebuzna. When all men say you are an ass, it is time to bray.
	65	Dijo el asno al mulo: anda para allá, orejudo. *Ill may the kiln call the oven burnt-tail.*
	66	El asno sufre la carga, pero no la sobrecarga. The ass endures his burden, but not more than his burden.

67 Más quiero asno que me lleve, que caballo que me derrueque.
    Better ride an ass that carries me than a horse that throws me.

68 Quien no puede dar en el asno, da en la albarda.
    He that cannot beat the ass, beats the saddle.

Atafea   69 Uno muere de atafea y otro la desea.
                   One man's fortune is another's misfortune.

Atajo   70 No hay atajo sin trabajo.
                   No pains, no gains. No sweet without sweat.

Ausente   71 Ni ausente sin culpa, ni presente sin disculpa.
                   The absent are always in the wrong.

Ave   72 Todas las aves con sus pares.
                   Birds of a feather flock together.

Avenencia 73 Más vale mala avenencia que buena sentencia.
                   Better an ill agreement than a good judgment.

Ayudarse   74 Ayúdate y el cielo te ayudará.
                   God helps those who help themselves.

Ayuno   75 El harto, de ayuno no tiene duelo.
                   He whose belly is full believes not him who is fasting.

B

Barato	76	Lo barato sale (es) caro. Good cheap is dear.
Barba	77	A barba de necio aprenden todos a rapar. A barber learns to shave by shaving fools.
	78	Cuando las barbas del vecino veas pelar, pon las tuyas a remojar. *When your neighbour's house is on fire, beware of your own.*
Bayo	79	Uno piensa el bayo y otro el que lo ensilla. One thing thinks the horse, another he that saddles him. *One thing thinks the bear, and another he that leads him.*
Beber	80	Después de beber, cada uno da su parecer. *What soberness conceals, drunkenness reveals.*
	81	Do entra beber, sale saber. When wine is in, wit is out.
Belleza	82	Belleza poco dura, más vale cordura. *Beauty is only skin-deep.*

83 Belleza sin bondad es como vino desbrebado.
A fair woman without virtue is like palled wine.

84 Belleza y locura van juntas a menudo.
Beauty and folly are old companions.

Beltrán 85 Quien bien quiere a Beltrán, bien quiere a su can.
Love me, love my dog.

Bestia 86 A bestia loca, recuero modorro.
A curst cur (dog) must be tied short. A boisterous horse must have a rough bridle.

87 A la bestia cargada el sobornal la mata.
The last straw will break the camel's back.

88 Quien bestia va a Roma, bestia retorna.
If an ass goes traveling, he'll not come back a horse.

Bien 89 Del bien al mal, no hay un canto de real.
From the sublime to the ridiculous is only a step. Extremes meet.

90 El bien no esconocido hasta que es perdido.
The worth of a thing is best known by its want.

91 El bien suena y el mal vuela.
Good news travels slowly, bad news travels fast.

92 Hacer bien, nunca se pierde.
A good deed is never lost.

Bobo 93 A los bobos (se les) aparece la Madre de Dios.
Fortune favours fools.

94 Bobos van al mercado, cada uno con su asno.
If all fools wore white caps, we'd all seem like geese.

95 El bobo, si es callado, por sesudo es reputado.
A fool who is silent is counted wise.

Boca	96	En boca cerrada no entra(n) mosca(s).s35
		A closed mouth catches no flies.
	97	Por la boca muere el pez.
		A fish wouldn't get caught if it kept its mouth shut.
	98	Quien tiene boca, no diga a otro "sopla."
		If you yourself can do it, attend no other's help or hand.
Bocado	99	No hay mejor bocado que el hurtado.
		Stolen waters (kisses) (pleasures) are sweet.
Bodega	100	La bodega huele al vino que tiene.
		Every cask smells of the wine it contains.
Bueno	101	Allégate a los buenos, y serás uno de ellos.
		Keep good men company, and you shall be of the number.
	102	Lo bueno cansa, y lo malo nunca se daña.
		I'd rather have a comfortable vice than a virtue that bores.
	103	Lo bueno fue, y lo malo es.
		Sorrow remains when joy is but a blast.
	104	Lo bueno, si breve, dos veces bueno.
		Brevity is the soul of wit.
	105	Nunca lo bueno fue mucho.
		What's good was never plentiful.
	106	Uno que es bueno, para sí es bueno.
		Do good, you do it for yourself.
Buey	107	Al buey por el cuerno (asta), y al hombre por el verbo (la palabra).
		An ox is taken by the horns, and a man by the tongue.

108   Buey viejo, surco derecho.
       An old ox makes a straight furrow.

109   El buey (caballo) harto no es comedor.
       When the cat is full, then the milk tastes sour.

110   El buey solo (suelto) bien se lame.
       An ox, when he is alone, licks himself at pleasure.

111   Entre bueyes, no hay cornadas.
       Dog will not eat dog.

112   Lo que ha de cantar el buey, canta la carreta.
       One who complains most suffers less.

Buhonero   113   Cada buhonero (uno) alaba sus agujas.
       Every peddlar praises his needles.

Buñolero   114   Buñolero, a tus buñuelos.
       Every man to his trade.

Burla   115   A la burla, dejarla cuando más agrada.
       When your jest is at its best, let it rest.

116   Las burlas se vuelven en veras.
       Jesters do oft prove prophets.

117   No hay peor burla que la verdadera.
       There is no worse jest than a true one.

Buscar   118   Quien busca halla.
       Seek and you shall find.

C

Caballero	119	A caballero nuevo, caballo viejo. A young trooper should have an old horse.
Caballo	120	A caballo regalado (presentado), no se le mira (no hay que mirarle) el diente. Don't look a gift horse in the mouth.
	121	Caballo que vuela no quiere espuela. Don't spur a willing horse.
	122	Caballo alquilado, nunca cansado. A hired horse never tires.
	123	El caballo que mucho anda, nunca falta quien le bata. *The horse that draws best is most whipped.*
	124	Se puede llevar el caballo al abrevadero, pero no obligarlo a beber. You can lead a horse to water, but you can't make him drink.
Cabello	125	Cada cabello hace su sombra en el suelo. *The smallest hair casts its shadow.*

Cabeza 126 Antes (más vale ser) cabeza de ratón, que cola de león.
Better be the head of a mouse than the tail of a lion.

127 Cuantas cabezas, tantos pareceres.
So many heads, so many wits.

128 El que no tiene cabeza, tiene que tener pies.
What you haven't got in your head, you have in your feet.

Cabo 129 El que está en muchos cabos, no está en ninguno.
He who begins many things, finishes but few.

Cabra 130 La cabra de mi vecina más leche da que la mía.
Our neighbour's ground yields better corn than ours.

131 La cabra siempre tira al monte.
The frog cannot out of her bog.

Caer 132 El que no cae no se levanta.
Who never climbed, never fell. Failure teaches success.

Caída 133 De muy alto, grandes caídas se dan.
The higher you climb, the harder you fall.

Calma 134 Gran calma, señal de agua.
There is always a calm before a storm.

Calumnia 135 Calumnia, que algo queda.
Slander leaves a score behind it.

Calza 136 A calza corta, agujeta longa (larga).
A little goes a long way. Little dogs have long tails.

Callar	137	Calle el que dio y hable el que tomó.
		Let him who gives be silent, and him who receives speak.
	138	Más vale callar que mal hablar.
		Be silent if you have nothing worth saying.
	139	Quien calla, otorga.
		Silence gives consent.
Cama	140	Quien mala cama hace, en ella se yace.
		As one makes his bed, so must he lie.
Camino	141	En luengo camino paja pesa.
		In a long journey, straw weighs.
	142	En luengos caminos se conocen amigos.
		In sports and journeys friends are known.
Camisa	143	Más cerca está la camisa de la carne que el jubón.
		Near is my coat, but nearer is my shirt.
	144	Primero es la camisa que el sayo.
		Near is my shirt, but nearer is my skin.
Campana	145	Campana cascada, nunca sana.
		A cracked bell can never sound well.
	146	Cual es la campana, tal la badajada.
		As the bell is, so is the clapper.
Can	147	Can con rabia a su dueño muerde.
		The mad dog bites his master.
	148	Can que mucho lame, saca sangre.
		Dogs begin in jest and end in earnest.
	149	Can viejo no ladra en vano.
		An old dog barks not in vain.

150   Canes que ladran, ni muerden ni toman caza.
*A barking dog never bites. A barking dog was never
a good hunter.*

151   Más vale can vivo que león muerto.
Better a live dog than a dead lion.

Canasta   152   Quien hace la canasta, hará el canastillo.
He that makes one basket can make a hundred.

Cantarillo   153   Cantarillo que muchas veces va a la fuente, o deja
el asa o la frente.
*A pitcher that goes to the well too often is broken at
last.*

Cántaro   154   Si da el cántaro en la piedra, o la piedra en el
cántaro, mal para el cántaro.
*Whether the pitcher strikes the stone or the stone
the pitcher, it is bad for the pitcher.*

Canto   155   Por el canto se conoce el pájaro.
A bird is known by his note.

Caña   156   Las cañas se vuelven lanzas.
It is ill jesting with edged tools.

Capa   157   A capa vieja no dan oreja.
A poor man's tale cannot be heard.

158   Debajo de una mala capa hay un buen bebedor.
Through tattered clothes small vices do appear.

159   Una buena capa todo lo tapa.
Good clothes open all doors.

Capilla   160   No son todos los que traen capilla frailes.
The cowl does not make the monk.

Capillo   161   Lo que en el capillo se toma y pega, con la
                       mortaja se deja.
                       What is learned in the cradle lasts till the grave.

Capitán   162   Donde manda capitán, no manda marinero.
                       Some must follow and some command.

Caridad   163   La caridad bien entendida (ordenada) empieza por
                       casa (uno mismo).
                       Charity begins at home.

Carne   164   La carne en el techo y la hambre en el pecho.
                       The ass loaded with gold still eats thistles.

                 165   No hay carne sin hueso.
                       Bones bring meat to town.

                 166   Quien come la carne, que roa el hueso.
                       He who eats the meat, let him pick the bone.

Carnero   167   Cada carnero cuelga de su piezgo.
                       Let every peddlar carry his own pack.

Carreta   168   Quien hace la carreta, sabrá deshacella.
                       What man makes, man can destroy.

Carro   169   Carro que rechina llega lejos.
                       A creaking door hangs long on its hinges.

                 170   Quien su carro unta, sus bueyes ayuda.
                       He who greases his wheels helps his oxen.

Casa   171   A mal decir, no hay casa fuerte.
                       No fence against a flail.

                 172   Beata la casa en que hay viejo cabe su brasa.
                       An old man in the house is a good sign.

173   Cada cual es rey en su casa.
      Every man is king in his home.

174   Casa con dos puertas mala es de guardar.
      The back door robs the house.

175   En casa del ahorcado, no hay que mentar la soga.
      Never mention a rope in the house of a man who
      has been hanged.

176   En casa del gaitero (tamborilero) todos son danzan-
      tes.
      In the house of a fiddler, all fiddle.

177   En casa del herrero, badil de madero (cuchillo de
      palo).
      *The blacksmith's horse and the shoemaker's family al-
      ways go unshod. The painter (paperhanger) never
      paints (papers) his own house.*

178   En casa del mezquino (hacino) (ruin), más manda
      la mujer que el marido (la mujer es alguacil).
      When a man's a fool, the wife will rule.

179   En casa llena, presto se guisa la cena.
      *They that have a good store of butter may lay it
      thick on their bread. In an orderly house, all things
      are always ready.*

180   La casa quemada, acudís con el agua.
      When the house is burned down, you bring water.

181   Por la casa se conoce al dueño.
      The house shows the owner.

182   Triste está la casa donde la gallina canta y el gallo
      calla.
      It's a sad house where the hen crows louder than
      the cock.

Casar   183   Antes que te cases, mira lo que haces.
              Before you marry, 'tis well to tarry.

184   Casar y compadrar, cada cual con su igual.
      Marry your like.

185   Quien casa por amores, malos días y buenas no-
      ches.
      *Who marries for love without money, has good nights
      and sorry days.*

Castigar   186   Quien a uno castiga, a ciento hostiga.
                     He who punishes one threatens a hundred.

Causa   187   Quitando la causa, cesa el efecto.
                  Take away the cause and the effect must cease.

Cautela   188   Buena cautela iguala buen consejo.
                    He is wise that is wary in time.

Cazar   189   El que dos liebres caza, a veces toma una, y
                  muchas veces, ninguna.
                  He who chases two hares catches neither.

            190   Uno levanta la caza y otro la mata.
                  One beats the bush and another catches the birds.

Cedazo   191   Cedacito nuevo, tres días en estaca.
                   New things are fair. Everything new is fine.

             192   Más quiero pedir a mi cedazo un pan apretado
                   que a mi vecina un pan prestado.
                   *Rather go to bed supperless than run in debt for a
                   breakfast.*

Celada   193   A celada de bellacos, más vale por los pies que por
                   las manos.
                   *The best remedy against an ill man is much ground
                   between.*

Cena	194	Acuéstate sin cena y amanecerás sin deuda.
		Better go to bed supperless than rise in debt.
	195	Más mató la cena que sanó Avicena.
		Gluttony kills more than the sword.
	196	Quien se echa sin cena, toda la noche devanea.
		Who goes to bed supperless, all night tumbles and tosses.
Centella	197	De pequeña centella se levanta gran fuego (grande hoguera).
		A little spark kindles a great fire.
Cepo	198	Afeita un cepo y parecerá un mancebo.
		Dress up a stick and it does not appear to be a stick.
Cerero	199	Al que ha de morir a oscuras, poco le importa ser cerero.
		He that is born to be hanged, shall never be drowned.
Cerradura	200	No hay cerradura donde es oro la ganzúa.
		The golden key opens every door.
Cesto	201	Quien hace un cesto, hará ciento.
		He that makes one basket can make a hundred.
Ciego	202	No hay peor ciego que el que no quiere ver.
		None are so blind as those who will not see.
	203	Si un ciego guía a otro ciego, ambos caerán en un (van a peligro de caer en el) hoyo.
		If the blind lead the blind, both shall fall into the ditch.
Cielo	204	El que al cielo escupe, en la cara le cae.
		Who spits against the wind, spits in his own face.

205   No es blando el camino del cielo.
      There is no going to heaven in a sedan.

Clavo   206   Por un clavo se pierde una herradura.
                 For want of a nail, the shoe was lost.

           207   Un clavo saca otro clavo.
                 One nail drives out another.

Codicia   208   La codicia rompe el saco.
                 Covetousness breaks the sack.

Cojera   209   En cojera de perro y en lágrimas de mujer, no hay
                 que creer.
                 It is no more pity to see a woman weep, than to see a
                 goose go barefoot.

Comenzar   210   Mejor es no comenzar lo que no se puede acabar.
                 Better never begin than never make an end.

Comer   211   Comer a gusto, y hablar y vestir al uso.
                 Eat to please yourself, but dress to please others.

           212   El comer y el rascar, todo es empezar.
                 Eating and scratching, it's all in the beginning.

           213   El que come más, come menos.
                 He that eats least, eats most.

           214   Se debe comer para vivir, no vivir para comer.
                 One should eat to live, not live to eat.

Comida   215   Comida hecha (el pan comido), compañía
                 deshecha.
                 The dinner over, away go the guests.

Comparación 216 Toda comparación es odiosa.
                 Comparisons are odious.

| Comprar | 217 | Quien compra lo que no puede, vende lo que le duele. |

Buy what you do not want and you will sell what you cannot spare.

| Común | 218 | Quien sirve al común, sirve a ningún. |

The best governed are least governed.

| Conciencia | 219 | La conciencia vale por mil testigos. |

Conscience is a thousand witnesses.

| | 220 | Una buena conciencia es una buena almohada. |

A clean conscience is a good pillow.

| Conejo | 221 | El conejo ido, el consejo venido. |

It is easy to be wise after the event. It's too late to shut the stable door after the horse has bolted.

| Confidencia | 222 | Confidencia quita reverencia. |

Familiarity breeds contempt.

| Consejo | 223 | A lo pasado, no hay consejo ninguno. |

Past cure, past care.

| | 224 | Al buen consejo, no se halla precio. |

Good advice is beyond price.

| | 225 | Consejo sin remedio es cuerpo sin alma. |

Good words without deeds are rushes and reeds.

| | 226 | El consejo de la mujer es poco, y el que no lo toma, un loco |

A woman's advice is no great thing, but he who won't take it is a fool.

| Contento | 227 | Una hora de contento paga cien años de tormento. |

One day of pleasure is worth two of sorrow.

Corazón	228	A donde el corazón se inclina, el pie camina. *Where your will is ready, your feet are light.*
	229	Buen corazón quebranta mala ventura. A stout heart crushes ill luck.
	230	De la abundancia del corazón habla la boca. *What the heart thinks, the tongue speaks.*
Cordero	231	Tan presto se va el cordero como el carnero. Death devours lambs as well as sheep.
Cordura	232	No templa cordura lo que destempla ventura. *An ounce of luck is worth a pound of wisdom.*
Cornudo	233	El cornudo es el postrero que lo sabe. *The husband is always the last to know.*
Corriente	234	No se debe ir contra la corriente. Strive not against the stream.
Corsario	235	De corsario a corsario no se pierden sino los barriles. *A crow doesn't pull out the eye of another crow.*
Cortesía	236	A mucha cortesía, mayor cuidado. *Too much courtesy, too much craft. Too much politeness is a form of cunning.*
	237	Cortesía de boca, gana mucho a poca costa. *Politeness costs nothing and gains everything.*
Cosa	238	Cada cosa en su tiempo. There is a time for everything.
	239	Cosa hallada no es hurtada. *Finding is keeping.*

240 El que no duda, no sabe cosa ninguna (nada).
He who doubts nothing knows nothing.

241 La cosa que es menos hallada, es más preciada.
The thing which is rare is dear.

242 No hay cosa más barata que la que se compra.
What is bought is cheaper than a gift.

243 No hay nada nuevo (cosa nueva) debajo del sol.
Nothing new under the sun.

244 No hay ninguna cosa tan escondida que no sea
sabida.
Nothing so secret but time and truth will reveal it.

245 Quien desalaba la cosa, ése la compra.
He that blames would buy.

246 Quien las cosas mucho apura, no tiene vida segura.
*He that pries into every cloud, may be stricken with
a thunderbolt.*

247 Tres cosas echan al hombre de casa fuera: el
humo, la gotera y la mujer vocinglera.
Three things drive a man out of his home: smoke,
rain, and a scolding wife.

Costar 248 Nunca mucho costó poco.
Much never costs little.

Costumbre 249 De malas costumbres nacen buenas leyes.
Good laws often proceed from bad manners.

250 La costumbre es otra (segunda) naturaleza.
Custom is almost a second nature.

251 La costumbre hace ley.
Customs are stronger than laws.

Criado	252	Quien ha criados, ha enemigos no excusados.
		So many servants, so many enemies.
Crítica	253	La crítica es fácil, el arte difícil.
		It is easier to be critical than correct.
Cruz	254	Cada cual lleva su cruz.
		Every man has his cross to bear.
	255	Detrás de la cruz está el diablo.
		The devil lurks behind the cross.
	256	La cruz en los pechos, y el diablo en los hechos.
		The devil can cite scripture for his purpose.
Cuba	257	Cada cuba huele al vino que tiene.
		Every cask smells of the wine it contains.
Cuchillada	258	Sanan cuchilladas (llagas), y no malas palabras.
		Words cut more than swords.
Cuchillo	259	No todos los que llevan largos cuchillos son verdugos.
		Not everyone who carries a long knife is a cook.
	260	Un cuchillo afila el otro.
		One knife sharpens another.
	261	Un cuchillo mesmo me parte el pan y me corta el dedo.
		The same knife cuts bread and fingers.
Cuenta	262	Cuentas claras (cuenta y razón) conservan la amistad.
		Short accounts make long friends.
Cuero	263	De cuero ajeno, correas largas.
		He is free of horse that never had one.

Cuervo   264   Cría cuervos, y te sacarán los ojos.
Nourish a snake in one's bosom.

265   Cual el cuervo, tal su huevo.
Of an evil crow, an evil egg.

266   No puede ser más negro el cuervo que sus alas.
Black will take no other hue.

Culantro   267   Bueno es el culantro, pero no tanto.
Enough is enough. Enough of a good thing is plenty.

Culpa   268   La culpa del asno echarla a la albarda.
The losing horse blames the saddle.

269   Por culpa de la bestia mataron al obispo.
One does the scathe and another has the scorn.

Cuna   270   Lo que se aprende en la cuna, siempre dura.
What is learned in the cradle lasts till the grave.

Cuña   271   Donde no valen cuñas, aprovechan uñas.
Cunning surpasses strength. If the lion's skin cannot, the fox's shall.

272   No hay peor cuña que la de la misma madera.
Nothing worse than a familiar enemy.

Cura   273   No se acuerda el cura de cuando fue sacristán.
The cow has forgotten she was once a calf.

274   Como te curas, duras.
He lives longest who lives best.

D

Dádiva	275	Dádiva ruineja, a su dueño semeja.
		A wicked man's gift has a touch of his master.
	276	Dádivas quebrantan peñas.
		The gift bringer always finds an open door.
Dado	277	Cuando te dieren el buen dado, échale la mano.
		Take while the taking is good.
Dar	278	Lo mejor de los dados es no jugarlos.
		The best throw of the dice is to throw them away.
	279	A quien dan en qué escoger, le dan en qué entender.
		Who has a choice, has trouble.
	280	Donde las dan las toman (El dar va con el tomar).
		Give and take. Give as good as one gets. Tit for tat.
	281	Nadie (ninguno) puede dar lo que no tiene.
		No one can give what he hasn't got.
	282	Quien da lo suyo antes de morir, prepárase a bien sufrir.
		He that gives his goods before he be dead, take up a mallet and knock him on the head.

	283	Quien presto da, dos veces da (La presta dádiva su efecto ha doblado). *He gives twice who gives quickly.*
Dátil	284	No hay dátil sin hueso, ni bien sin lacerio. *He that would eat the kernel must crack the nut.*
Decir	285	Decir y hacer no comen a una mesa. *Saying and doing are two things.*
	286	Del decir al hacer mucho hay (Del dicho al hecho hay gran trecho). *From word to deed is a great space.*
	287	Dime con quien andas, te diré quién eres. *Tell me with whom you travel and I'll tell you who you are.*
	288	Presto es dicho lo que es bien dicho. *Speak little, speak well.*
	289	Quien dice lo que no debe, oye lo que no quiere. *He that speaks the thing he should not, hears the thing he would not.*
	290	Quien mal dice, peor oye. *He who speaks evil, hears worse.*
Dedo	291	Los dedos de la mano no son iguales. *No like is the same.*
Demora	292	Toda demora es peligrosa. *Delays are dangerous.*
Deseo	293	El deseo hace hermoso lo feo. *Love sees no faults.*
	294	Los deseos no llenan el saco. *Wishes never fill the bag.*

Destruir	295	Es más fácil destruir que construir.
		It's easier to pull down than to build up.

Deuda	296	Quien fía o promete, en deuda se mete.
		A promise is a debt. A promise made is a debt unpaid.

Día	297	Cada día gallina (olla) amarga la cocina (el caldo).
		Too much of ought is good for nought. Too much honey cloys the stomach.
	298	Día de mucho, víspera de nada.
		If you sing before breakfast, you'll cry before night.
	299	El día que te casas, o te curas o te matas.
		Marriage makes or mars a man.
	300	No hay día tan lueñe que presto no esté presente.
		Never think of the future, it comes soon enough.
	301	Quien tarde se levanta, todo el día trota.
		He that rises late must trot all day.
	302	Vale más un día del hombre discreto, que toda la vida del necio.
		It is better to live like a lion for a day than to live like a lamb for a hundred years.

Diablo	303	Cuando el diablo reza, engañarte quiere.
		When the fox preaches, beware your geese.
	304	El diablo, harto de carne, se metió a fraile.
		When all is consumed, repentance comes too late. The end of passion is the beginning of repentance.
	305	El diablo sabe por diablo, pero más sabe por viejo (más sabe el diablo por ser viejo que por ser diablo).
		The devil knows many things because he is old.

306   Nunca el diablo hizo empanada de que no quisiese
       comer la mejor parte.
       When the devil prays, he has booty in his eye.

Diente   307   Cuando pienses meter el diente en seguro, toparás
       en duro.
       He that is too secure is not safe.

308   Primero son mis dientes que mis parientes.
       *Near is my shirt, but nearer is my skin. Number one
       is the first house in the row.*

Dieta   309   Más cura la dieta que la lanceta.
       Diet cures more than the doctor.

Dificultad   310   No hay mayor dificultad que la poca voluntad.
       Nothing is easy to the unwilling.

Diligencia   311   La diligencia es madre de la buena ventura.
       Diligence is the mother of good fortune.

Dinero   312   A dineros dados (pagados), brazos quebrados.
       *The money paid, the work delayed. Pay beforehand
       and your work will be behindhand.*

313   Dinero llama dinero.
       Money begets (draws) (makes) money.

314   El dinero es buen servidor y mal amo.
       Money is a good servant but a bad master.

315   El dinero es el nervio de la guerra.
       Money is the sinews of war.

316   El dinero es redondo para rodar.
       Money is round and rolls away.

317 El dinero gobierna el mundo.
Money makes the world go round. Money runs the world.

318 El dinero hace al hombre entero.
Money makes a man free.

319 El dinero nunca se goza hasta que se gasta.
The value of money lies in what we do with it.

320 En cuanto hay dinero, hay amigos.
Rich folk have many friends.

321 Si no tienes dinero en la bolsa, ten miel en la boca.
He that has no honey in his pot, let him have it in his mouth.

Dios

322 A quien Dios quiere ayudar, nada le puede perjudicar.
Where God will help, nothing does harm.

323 A quien Dios quiere bien, la perra le pare lechones.
Whom God loves, his bitch brings forth pigs.

324 A quien Dios quiere, la casa le sube.
Well thrives he whom God loves.

325 Ayúdate bien, y ayudarte ha Dios.
God helps those who help themselves.

326 Con lo mío me ayude Dios.
God reaches us good things by our own hands.

327 Cuando Dios no quiere, lo santos no pueden.
When it pleases not God, the saint can do little.

328 Cuando Dios quiere, con todos aires llueve.
When God will, no wind but brings rain.

329 Da Dios almendras al que no tiene muelas.
The gods send nuts to those who have no teeth.

330   Dios aprieta, pero no ahoga.
God grips but does not choke.

331   Dios da el frío conforme la ropa.
God sends cold after clothes.

332   Dios es el que sana, y el médico lleva la plata.
God heals and the doctor takes the fee.

333   Dios me guarde del agua mansa, que yo me libraré de la brava.
God defend me from my friends; from my enemies I can defend myself.

334   Dios me libre de hombre de un libro.
God protect us from him who has read but one book.

335   Dios, que da la llaga, da la medicina.
The hand that gave the wound must give the cure.

336   Más vale a quien Dios ayuda, que quien mucho madruga.
God's help is better than early rising.

337   No hiere Dios con dos manos (que a la mar hizo puertos y a los ríos vados).
God strikes not with both hands (for to the sea he made havens, and to rivers fords).

338   Quien se guarda, Dios le guarda.
God helps him who helps himself.

339   Quien se muda, Dios le ayuda.
God aids him who changes.

Discreto   340   Mientras el discreto piensa, el necio hace la ciencia.
A fool talks while a wise man thinks. A wise man knows his own ignorance, a fool thinks he knows.

Doblar   341   Antes doblar que quebrar.
Better bend than break.

Doctor	342	Donde hay más doctores, hay más dolores. The more doctors, the more diseases.
Dormir	343	Mucho dormir causa mal vestir. *Sloth breeds poverty.*
Dos	344	Cuando dos pleitean, un tercero saca provecho. *Two dogs fight over a bone while the third runs away with it.*
Ducado	345	Si quieres saber lo que vale un ducado pídele prestado. If you would know the value of a ducat, try to borrow one.
Duelo	346	Los duelos con pan son menos (buenos). All griefs with bread are less.
Dueño	347	Cual el dueño, tal el perro. As the master is, so is his dog.
Dulce	348	A nadie le amarga un dulce. *Everyone fastens where there is gain.*
Duro	349	Duro con duro no hacen buen muro. Hard and hard makes not the stone wall.

E

Ejercicio   350   El ejercicio hace maestro.
Practice makes perfect. Use makes mastery.

Empezar   351   Lo que no se empieza, no se acaba.
Where there's no beginning, there's no end.

Encuentro   352   Al mal encuentro, darle de mano y mudar asiento.
The best remedy against an ill man is much ground between.

Enemigo   353   A enemigo que huye, puente de plata.
For a flying enemy, make a golden bridge.

354   No hay enemigo pequeño.
There is no little enemy.

355   Quien a su enemigo popa, a sus manos muere.
He that dallies with an enemy, dies by his own hand.

Engañar   356   Aquél es engañado quien cuida engañar a otro.
If you dig a pit for someone else, you fall into it yourself.

Enseñar   357   Enseñando, aprendemos.
One learns by teaching.

Entendedor	358	A buen entendedor, pocas palabras (breve hablador). A word to the wise is sufficient.
Errar	359	Malo es errar, y peor es perseverar. *We all err, but only fools continue in error.*
Error	360	Los errores de los médicos, la tierra los cubre. The doctor's errors are covered by earth.
Escaño	361	Alguno está en el escaño, que a sí no aprovecha y a otro hace daño. *The dog in the manger won't eat oats nor let anyone else eat them.*
Escarbar	362	Muchas veces, el que escarba, lo que no quería halla. *He that peeps through a hole, may see what will vex him. He that pries into every cloud, may be stricken with a thunderbolt.*
Escarmentar	363	De los escarmentados nacen los arteros. *Trouble brings experience and experience brings wisdom.*
	364	El escarmentado bien conoce el vado. *An old ox will find shelter for himself.*
Escaso	365	Más gasta el escaso que el franco. The covetous spend more than the liberal.
Escribano	366	El mejor escribano echa un borrón. *Even Homer sometimes nods.*
Espalda	367	Espaldas vueltas, memorias muertas. *Long absent, soon forgotten. Out of sight, out of mind.*

	368	Sólo se conoce el bien por las espaldas. *Good is recognized when it goes, and evil when it comes.*
Especie	369	Ofrecer mucho al que poco pide, es especie de negar. *To offer much is a kind of denial.*
Esperanza	370	Más vale buena esperanza que ruin posesión. A good hope is better than a bad possession.
Esperar	371	El que esperar puede, obtiene lo que quiere. Everything comes to him who waits.
	372	Quien espera, desespera. Too much hope deceives.
Espina	373	La espina cuando nace, la punta lleva delante. It early pricks that will be a thorn.
Estar	374	El que bien está no se mueva (mude). *Don't change horses in midstream. We do not always gain by changing.*
Estatua	375	A gran estatua, gran basa. *High things must have low foundations. Great ships need deep waters.*
Estrella	376	Unos nacen con estrella, y otros nacen estrellados. *Some of us have the hap, others stick in the gap.*
Experiencia	377	La experiencia es madre de la ciencia. Experience is the mother of wisdom.
Extremo	378	Los extremos se tocan. Extremes meet.

F

Falta 379 A falta de caldo, buena es la carne.
Gnaw the bone which is fallen to your lot.

379... 380 A falta de hombres buenos, a mi padre hicieron alcalde.
In the land of the blind, the one-eyed are kings.

381 A falta de pan, buenas son tortas.
Lacking bread, tarts are good.
If they can't eat bread, let them eat cake.

382 A falta de pollo, pan y cebolla.
If you have not a capon, feed on an onion.

Fama 383 Buena fama hurto encubre.
A good reputation covers a multitude of sins.

384 Cobra buena fama, y échate a dormir.
Win a good reputation and sleep at your ease.

385 Más vale buena fama que dorada cama.
A good name is better than riches.

386 Unos tienen la fama y otros cardan la lana.
Some have the fame, and others live in shame.

Favo 387 El favo es dulce, mas pica la abeja.
Honey is sweet, but bees sting.

Feria   388   Cada uno cuenta de la feria como le va en ella.
                        No dish pleases all palates alike. Everyone speaks for
                        his own interest.

Figura   389   Hoy figura, mañana sepultura.
                        Today a man, tomorrow none.

Fin   390   A la fin loa la vida, y a la tarde loa el día.
                        Praise a fine (fair) day at night. Praise no man till
                        he is dead.

                 391   Al fin se canta la gloria.
                        Do not halloo till you're out of the wood.

                 392   El fin corona la obra.
                        The end crowns the work.

                 393   El fin justifica los medios.
                        The end justifies the means.

                 394   Hasta el fin nadie es dichoso.
                        Call no man happy till he dies.

Fortuna   395   Cuanto mayor es la fortuna, tanto es menos segura.
                        Great happiness, great danger.

                 396   Harto bien baila, a quien la fortuna suena.
                        He dances well to whom fortune pipes.

                 397   La fortuna es de vidrio, cuanto más brilla más
                        frágil es.
                        Fortune is like glass: it breaks when it is brightest.

                 398   No puede la fortuna quitar lo que no dio.
                        Fortune can take nothing from us but what she
                        has given.

Fruta   399   Uno come la fruta aceda, y otro tiene la dentera.
                        Adam ate the apple and our teeth still ache.

Fuego	400	Donde fuego se hace, humo sale.

There's no smoke without fire.

	401	Si el fuego está cerca de la estopa, llega el diablo y sopla.

Man is straw, woman fire - and the devil blows.

Fuerte	402	Acometa quienquiera, el fuerte espera.

Fools rush in where wise men fear to tread.
Discretion is the better part of valour.

Fuerza	403	A fuerza de varón, espada de gorrión.

A brave arm makes a short sword long.

	404	Donde fuerza viene, derecho se pierde.

Where force prevails, right perishes.

G

Galgo	405	A la larga, el galgo a la liebre mata. *At length the fox is brought to the furrier.*
Gallina	406	A veces una gallina ciega encuentra su grano. *A blind man may sometimes hit the mark.*
	407	La gallina de mi vecina más huevos pone que la mía. *Our neighbour's ground yields better corn than ours.*
	408	La gallina negra pone el huevo blanco. A black hen always lays a white egg.
Gallo	409	Cada gallo canta en su muladar. *Every cock crows loudest on his own dunghill.*
	410	El que solo come su gallo, solo ensilla su caballo. He who eats his cock alone, must saddle his horse alone.
	411	No cantan bien dos gallos en un gallinero. *Two sparrows on one ear of corn make an ill agreement.*
Gana	412	Donde hay gana, hay maña. Where there's a will there's a way.

Ganado   413   Entre ruin ganado poco hay que escoger.
There's small choice among rotten apples. No choice among stinking fish.

414   No dejes lo ganado por lo que has de ganar.
Better keep now than seek anon. We would be better off to have than to have coming. A little thing in hand is worth more than a great thing in prospect.

Ganancia   415   Quien está de ganancia, no baraje.
Don't change horses in midstream.

Gandul   416   Para los gandules cada día es fiesta.
Every day is a holiday with sluggards.

Gastar   417   El que gasta poco, gasta doblado.
Good cheap is dear. Cheap goods always prove expensive.

Gato   418   Cuando el gato no está, los ratones bailan. (Vanse los gatos y entiéndense los ratos.)
When the cat's away, the mice will play.

419   El gato maullador, nunca buen cazador.
Muffled cats are not good mousers. The ass that brays most eats least.

420   Gato con guantes no caza ratones.
A cat in gloves catches no mice.

421   Gato escaldado, del agua fría ha miedo.
Scalded cats fear even cold water.

Gloria   422   Con las glorias se olvidan las memorias.
When glory comes, memory departs.

423   Gloria vana, florece y no grana.
Vainglory blossoms but never bears.

Golondrina	424	Una golondrina no hace verano. *One swallow does not make a summer.*
Gota	425	Gota a gota, la mar se apoca. *Many drops of water will sink a ship.*
Gotera	426	La gotera cava la piedra. *Constant dripping wears away the stone.*
	427	Quien no adoba gotera, hace casa entera. *A small leak will sink a ship.*
Grajo	428	Le dijo el grajo al cuervo: quítate allá, que tiznas. *The pot calls the kettle black. The snite need not the woodcock betwite.*
Grano	429	De un grano de agraz se hace mucha dentera. *One ill weed mars a whole pot of porridge.*
	430	Grano a grano, allega para tu año. *Little and often fills the purse.*
	431	Grano a grano, hinche la gallina el papo. *Grain by grain, and the hen fills her belly.*
	432	Más vale grano de pimienta que libra de arroz. *An ounce of fortune is worth a pound of forecast. Better to be a little wheel turning than a big one standing still.*
	433	Un grano no hace granero, pero ayuda a su compañero. *One grain fills not a sack but helps his fellow.*
Grey	434	La grey paga las locuras de su rey. *The pleasures of the mighty are the tears of the poor.*
Grumo	435	Grumos de oro llama el escarabajo a sus hijos. *The owl thinks her own young fairest.*

| Guardar | 436 | Quien guarda, halla. |
| | | *Hiders make the best finders. Of saving comes having.* |

| Guerra | 437 | El que tonto va a la guerra, tonto viene de ella. |
| | | *Send a fool to France (the market) and he'll come back a fool.* |

| | 438 | Ir a la guerra ni casar, no se ha de aconsejar. |
| | | Advise none to marry or to go to war. |

| | 439 | Quien no sabe qué es guerra, vaya a ella. |
| | | *War is sweet to them that know it not.* |

| Gula | 440 | Más mató la gula que la espada. |
| | | Gluttony kills more than the sword. |

| Gusto | 441 | Al gusto dañado, lo dulce le es amargo. |
| | | *A blind man can judge no colours. Bad eyes never see any good.* |

| | 442 | De gustos no hay disputa (nada escrito). |
| | | There is no disputing (accounting) for taste. |

H

Haba	443	Más quiero roer haba seguro y en paz, que comer mil manjares corrido y sin solaz. *It is better to have beans and bacon in peace than cakes and ale in fear. A crust of bread in peace is better than a feast in contention.*
Haber	444	El que no ha, no da. *There's no use trying to strip a naked man.*
Habilidad	445	La habilidad del artífice se conoce en su obra. *The workman is known by his work.*
Hábito	446	El hábito no hace al monje. The habit (cowl) does not make the monk.
Hablar	447	Cada uno habla como quien es. *A man's conversation is the mirror of his thoughts.*
	448	El poco hablar es oro y el mucho (hablar) es lodo. *Speech is silver, silence is golden.*
	449	Quien mucho habla, mucho yerra. *Talk much, and err much.*
Hacer	450	Hacientes y conscientes merecen igual pena. *The receiver is as bad as the thief.*

451 Haz tú lo que bien digo, y no lo que mal hago.
Do as I say, not as I do.

452 Quien tal hace, tal prenda.
The deed comes back upon the doer. If you give a jest, you must take a jest.

Hacienda 453 Quien da su hacienda antes de la muerte, merece que le den con un mazo en la frente.
He that gives his goods before he is dead, take a mallet and knock him on the head.

Hambre 454 A buen(a) hambre no hay pan duro, ni falta salsa a ninguno.
Hunger never saw bad bread (food).

455 El hambre echa el lobo del monte.
Hunger drives the wolf out of the wood.

456 Hambre y esperar, hacen rabiar.
A hungry man is an angry man.

457 Hambre y frío entregan al hombre a su enemigo.
Hunger and cold deliver a man up to his enemy.

458 Más vale una hartada que dos hambres.
Better belly burst than good meat.

Hecho 459 A lo hecho, pecho.
What's done cannot be undone.

460 A nuevos hechos, nuevos consejos.
New lords, new laws.

461 El que no quiere aventurar, no puede gran hecho acabar.
Nothing ventured, nothing gained.

462   Quien ha las hechas, ha las sospechas.
      A thief thinks that everyone else is a thief.

Herida   463   Quien dio la herida, la cura.
                    The hand that gave the wound must give the cure.

Hermano   464   Entre dos hermanos (hermano y hermano), un
                    notario y dos testigos (dos testigos y un escribano).
                    Between two brothers have two witnesses and a
                    voting.

Hiel   465   Poca hiel hace amarga mucha miel.
                    A drop of poison infects the whole tun of wine.

Hienda   466   Quien hienda echa en la coladera, hienda saca de
                    ella.
                    Garbage in, garbage out. If better were within,
                    better would come out.

Hierba   467   (La) mala hierba (cosa mala) nunca muere (crece
                    mucho).
                    Ill weeds grow apace.

              468   Mientras la hierba crece, el caballo muere.
                    While the grass grows, the horse starves.

Hierro   469   Quien a hierro mata, a hierro muere.
                    Who lives by the sword, dies by the sword.

Hígado   470   Lo que es bueno para el hígado, es malo para el
                    bazo.
                    Good for the liver may be bad for the spleen.

Higo   471   En tiempo de higos hay amigos.
                    Feast and your halls are crowded.

Hija   472   Muchas hijas en casa, todo se abrasa.
Two daughters and a back door are three arrant thieves.

473   Quien quiere la hija, halague la madre.
Who the daughter would win, with mama must begin.

Hijo   474   El hijo de la cabra, cabrito ha de ser.
The litter is like to the sire and dam.

475   El hijo de la gata, ratones mata.
The son of a cat pursues the rat.

476   El hijo sabe, que conoce a su padre.
It is a wise child that knows its own father.

Hilandera   477   A la mala hilandera, la rueca le hace dentera.
A bad shearer never had a good sickle.

Hilo   478   El hilo se corta (la cuerda se rompe) (se quiebra la soga) por lo más delgado (flojo).
The thread breaks where it is thinnest.

479   Por el hilo se saca el ovillo.
By the thread the ball is brought to light.

Hombre   480   Al hombre harto, las cerezas le amargan.
When the cat is full, the milk tastes sour.

481   Cuantos hombres, tantos pareceres.
So many men, so many minds.

482   De hombres es errar, de bestias perseverar en el error.
To err is human, to persist is beastly.

483   De los hombres se hacen obispos.
Bishops are made of men.
Nobody is born learned.

484 El hombre en la plaza, y la mujer en la casa.
     A woman's place is in the home.

485 El hombre es un lobo para el hombre.
     Man is to man a wolf.

486 El hombre propone y Dios dispone.
     Man proposes, God disposes.

487 Guárdate de hombre que no habla y de can que
     no ladra.
     Beware of a silent dog and silent water.

488 Hombre honrado, antes muerto que injuriado.
     *The brave man holds honour far more precious than
     life. It's better to die with honour than to live in in-
     famy.*

489 Hombre lento jamás tiene tiempo.
     Idle folks have the least leisure.

490 Hombre perezoso, en la fiesta es acucioso.
     Lazy folks' stomachs don't get tired.

491 Hombre prevenido vale por dos.
     Forewarned is forearmed.

492 Más vale perderse el hombre que perder el nombre.
     *A man may be deprived of life, but a good name
     can't be taken from him.*

493 No hay hombre sin hombre.
     *One man, no man. A man cannot live to himself
     alone.*

494 Siempre halla el hombre lo que no busca.
     Least expected, sure to happen.

495 Un hombre ocioso es la almohada del diablo.
     An idle person is the devil's cushion.

Homero 496 De vez en cuando dormita el gran Homero.
Even Homer sometimes nods.

Honor 497 El honor sostiene las artes.
Honours nourish arts.

498 Honores cambian costumbres.
Honours change manners.

Honra 499 Honra y provecho no caben en un saco.
Honour and profit do not lie in one sac.

Hora 500 Antes de la hora, gran denuedo; venidos al punto, mucho miedo.
Who takes a lion when he is absent, fears a mouse present.

501 Una hora suele quitar lo que en mil años se gana.
An hour may destroy what was an age in building.

Hormiga 502 Cada hormiga (mosca) tiene su ira (sombra).
The fly has her spleen, and the ant her gall.

Hornero 503 No seáis hornero(a) si tenéis la cabeza de manteca.
If your head is wax, do not walk in the sun. If you don't like the heat, get out of the kitchen.

Hueso 504 El que se traga un hueso, confianza tiene en su pescuezo.
A man must not swallow more than he can digest.

505 Quien te da un hueso, no te querría ver muerto.
He that gives you a bone, would not have you die.

Huésped 506 El huésped y el pece (pez) (pescado), a los tres días hiede.
Fish and guests smell in three days.

507 Huésped con sol, ha honor.
A golden key opens every door. A man's gift makes room for him.

Huir 508 Más vale huir que morir.
Better to be a coward for a minute than dead the rest of your life.

Hurtar 509 Quien una vez hurta, fiel nunca.
Once a thief, ever a thief.

I

Iglesia   510   Cerca de la iglesia, lejos de Dios.
                       The nearer the church, the farther from God.

Imposible   511   Nadie está obligado a lo imposible.
                       No one is bound to do the impossible.

Incierto   512   En busca de lo incierto, perdemos lo seguro.
                       Never quit certainty for hope.

Infierno   513   El infierno está lleno de buenos deseos, y el cielo
                       de buenas obras.
                       Hell is full of good meanings and wishes, but
                       heaven is full of good works.

Intención   514   De buenas intenciones está empedrado el infierno.
                       Hell is paved with good intentions.

Interés   515   Por el interés, lo más feo hermoso es.
                       Gain bends one's better judgment.

                 516   Quien bien va, no tuerce.
                       *Be sure you can better your condition before you
                       make a change. Don't change horses in the middle of
                       the stream. If it isn't broken, don't fix it.*

Ira

517 Donde acaba la ira comienza el arrepentimiento.
Anger begins with folly and ends with repentance.

518 Ira de enamorados, amores doblados.
The quarrel of lovers is the renewal of love.

519 Ira de hermanos, ira de diablos.
The wrath of brothers is the wrath of devils.

520 La ira es mala consejera.
Anger and haste hinder good counsel.

J

Juego   521   Afortunado en el juego, desgraciado en amores.
                    Lucky at cards, unlucky in love.

Justicia 522   Justicia extrema, extrema injusticia.
                    Extreme justice is extreme injustice.

              523   Justicia, mas no por mi casa.
                    *We all love justice, at our neighbour's expense. You
                    don't like justice when it is brought home to your
                    own doorstep.*

Juzgar   524   Quien a otro quiere juzgar, en sí debe comenzar.
                    *Judge well yourself before you criticize. Judge others
                    by what you do.*

L

Ladrón	525	El pequeño ladrón acaba encerrado, y el gran ladrón es ensalzado. Little thieves are hanged, great ones are honoured.
	526	Ladroncillo de agujeta, despés sube a barjuleta. *He that will steal a pin will steal a better thing.*
	527	Piensa el ladrón que todos son de su condición. The thief thinks that everyone else is a thief.
Lana	528	Cual más, cual menos, toda la lana es pelos. *There's small choice in rotten apples.*
	529	Ir por lana y volver trasquilado. Many go out for wool and come home shorn.
Lástima	530	Quien no quiera ver lástimas, no vaya a la guerra. *He that is afraid of wounds must not come near a battle.*
Lazo	531	Quien lazo me armó, en él cayó. *He who digs a pit for someone else, falls into it himself.*
Lengua	532	Allá va la lengua do duele la muela. The tongue returns to the aching tooth.

533 No diga la lengua (boca) lo que pague la cabeza (coca).
The tongue talks at the head's cost.

534 Quien lengua ha, a Roma va.
He who uses his tongue shall reach his destination.

Leña 535 La leña torcida da fuego recto.
Crooked logs make straight fires.

León 536 No es tan bravo el león como lo pintan.
The lion is not so fierce as he is painted.

Ley 537 El que hace la ley debe observarla.
Lawmakers shouldn't be lawbreakers.

538 Hecha la ley, hecha la trampa.
Every law has a loophole.

Libro 539 Libro cerrado no saca letrado.
A book that is shut is but a block.

Liebre 540 No se cazan liebres al son del tambor.
A hare is not caught with a drum.

Lobo 541 Con un lobo no se mata otro.
Two wrongs don't make a right.

542 Cuando el lobo va a hurtar, lejos de casa va a cazar.
The wolf preys farthest from his den.

543 Del lobo, un pelo.
You can have no more of a fox (cat) than her skin.

544 El lobo y la vulpeja, ambos son de una conseja.
The wolf and fox are both of one counsel.

545 Muda el lobo los dientes, y no las mientes.
Wolves may lose their teeth, but they never lose their nature.

546 Quien con lobos anda, a aullar se enseña.
He who goes with wolves will learn to howl.

547 Un lobo a otro no se muerden.
Wolves never prey upon wolves.

Loco 548 Cada loco con su tema.
Every man is mad on some point.

549 Cada uno lleva un loco en la manga.
Every man has a fool up his sleeve.

550 El loco, por la pena es cuerdo.
Experience is the mistress of fools.

551 Más sabe el loco en su casa que el cuerdo en la ajena.
A fool knows more in his own house than a wise man in another's.

552 Un loco hace ciento.
One fool makes many.

Locura 553 Quien de locura enferma, tarde o nunca sana.
Folly is an incurable disease.

554 Si la locura fuese dolores, en cada casa habría voces.
If all fools wore white caps, we'd all look like geese.

Luchar 555 Quien no lucha, no cae.
Who never climbed, never fell.

Luz 556 El que obra mal, detesta la luz (claridad).
He that does ill hates the light.

Ll

Llaga 557 La mala llaga sana, la mala fama mata.
An ill wound is cured, but not an ill name.

Llamar 558 Muchos son los llamados y pocos los escogidos.
Many are called, but few are chosen.

Llano 559 Aquel va más sano, que anda por el llano.
The beaten road is the safest. The safe way is the right way. It is safe riding in a good haven.

Llave 560 Las llaves en la cinta, y el perro en la cocina.
He that is secure is not safe.

561 Más vale vuelta de llave que consejo de fraile.
Put your trust in God but keep your powder dry.

Llegar 562 El primero que llega, ése la calza.
First come, first served. He that comes first to the hill, may sit where he will.

Llorar 563 El que no llora no mama.
The squeaking wheel gets the grease. The lame tongue gets nothing.

564 Llórame solo, y no me llores pobre.
It is better to want meat than guests or company.

M

Madera   565   La madera que nace para cuñas no admite
                   pulimento.
                   You cannot make a silk purse out of a sow's ear.

             566   No de toda madera pueden hacerse santos.
                   Every block is not a Mercury.

Madrastra 567   Madrastra, el nombre le basta.
                     Take heed of a stepmother, the very name of her
                     suffices.

Madre   568   Cual la madre, tal la hija (y tal la manta que las
                   cobija).
                   Like mother, like daughter.

             569   La buena madre no dice: "¿quieres?"
                   A good mother asks not "will you?" but gives.

             570   Madre piadosa hace hija asquerosa.
                   A pitiful mother makes a scabby daughter.

             571   Quien no cree en buena madre, creerá en mala
                   madrastra.
                   If you don't obey your mother, you will obey your
                   stepmother.

Maestro   572   Cada maestrillo tiene su librillo.
                    Every man in his own way.

573 Muchos maestros (componedores) cohonden (descomponen) la novia.
Too many cooks spoil the broth.

574 Nadie nace maestro.
Masters are made, not born.

575 No hay mejor maestro que el hambre.
Hunger tames the wild beast.

Mal

576 A chico mal, más trapo.
They complain most who suffer least.

577 A grandes males, grandes remedios.
Desperate evils require desperate remedies.

578 A mal hecho, ruego y pecho.
Admitting error clears the score and proves you wiser than before.

579 Allá va el mal, donde más hay.
Troubles (misfortunes) (misery) (sorrow) never come singly.

580 Ataja el mal en sus comienzos.
Destroy the lion while he is yet but a whelp. A stitch in time saves nine. Destroy the seed of evil, or it will grow up to your ruin.

581 Bien vengas, mal, si vienes solo.
Welcome evil (mischief), if you come alone.
Evil seldom goes alone.

582 Del mal, el menor.
Choose the lesser of two evils.

583 El mal entra a brazadas y sale a pulgaradas.
Misfortune arrives on horseback but departs on foot.
Misfortunes come on wings but depart on foot.

584 El mal llama al mal.
One evil breeds another.

585 En mal de muerte no hay médico que acierte.
*Death defies the doctor. There is a remedy for every-
thing but death.*

586 Haces mal, espera otro tal.
*Where vice is, vengeance follows. Old sins cast long
shadows.*

587 Mal ajeno del pelo cuelga.
We can always bear our neighbour's misfortunes.

588 Mal de muchos, consuelo de todos (tontos) (gozo
es).
Misery loves company.

589 Mal haya el romero que dice mal de su bordón.
*A bad workman quarrels with his tools. A bad
shearer never had a good sickle.*

590 Más mal hay en la aldehuela del que suena.
Things are not always what they seem.

591 No hay mal ni bien que cien años dure.
It will all be the same a hundred years hence.

592 No hay mal que por bien no venga.
Nothing but is good for something.

593 Piensa mal y acertarás.
Wise distrust is the parent of security.

594s90 Por su mal crió Dios alas a la hormiga.
*The ant had wings to her hurt. Ants live safely till
they have gotten wings.*

595 Quien canta, sus males espanta.
He who sings, drives away his cares.

596 Quien escucha, su mal oye.
Listeners hear no good of themselves.

597 Quien mal anda, mal acaba.
An ill life, an ill end.

598   Si el mal no fuese sentido, el bien no sería cono-
       cido.
       One doesn't appreciate happiness unless one has
       known sorrow.

Malo   599   El malo, para mal hacer, achaques no ha menester.
                       Any excuse will serve a tyrant. Wrong has no warrant.

                600   El malo siempre piensa engaño (ser engañado).
                       Ill-doers are ill-thinkers (deemers). Evil doers are evil
                       dreaders.

                601   Más vale malo conocido que bueno por conocer.
                       Better to bear the ills we have than fly to others that
                       we know not of.

Manga   602   Buenas son mangas después de Pascuas.
                       It's never too late to do good.

Manjar   603   No hay manjar que no empalague, ni vicio que no
                       enfade.
                       Too much of ought is good for nought.

                604   Un manjar solo continuo, presto pone hastío.
                       Too much honey cloys the stomach.

Mano   605   De la mano a la boca se pierde la sopa.
                       There's many a slip 'twixt the cup and the lip.

                606   De ruin mano, ruin dado.
                       A wicked man's gift has a touch of his master. Gifts
                       from enemies are dangerous.

                607   La mano cuerda no hace todo lo que dice la len-
                       gua.
                       A long tongue has a short hand.

                608   Manos besa el hombre que quisiera ver cortadas.
                       Many kiss the hand they wish to see cut off.

609   Manos blancas no ofenden.
       White hands cannot hurt.

610   Muchas manos en un plato, hacen ligero el trabajo
       (pronto tocan a rebato).
       Many hands make light work.

611   Por lo perdido no estés mano en mejilla.
       For a lost thing, care not.

612   Quien a mano ajena espera, mal yanta y peor cena.
       He who depends on another dines ill and sups
       worse.

613   Una mano lava la otra, y ambas la cara.
       One hand washes the other, and both the face.

Manzana   614   La manzana podrida pierde a su compañía.
                  One bad apple spoils the lot.

Maña   615   Más vale maña que fuerza.
                  Cunning is more than strength.

Mar   616   Hablar de la mar, y en ella no entrar.
                  Praise the sea, but keep on land.

           617   Quien no se aventura no pasa la mar.
                  He that will not sail till all the dangers are over
                  must not put to sea.

           618   Si quieres aprender a orar, entra en la mar.
                  He that will learn to pray, let him go to sea.

Marta   619   Bien canta Marta cuando está harta.
                  He dances well to whom fortune pipes.

Mata   620   De mala mata, nunca buena zarza (caza).
                  Of evil grain, no good seed can come. One cannot
                  gather grapes of thorns nor figs of thistles.

Matrimonio 621 Matrimonio y mortaja, del cielo baja.
Marriage and hanging go by destiny.

Mazo 622 Pescar con mazo no es renta cierta.
You can't saw wood with a hammer.

Medalla 623 Toda medalla tiene su reverso.
Every medal has its reverse.

Médico 624 Al médico y al letrado, no le quieras engañado.
Always tell your doctor and lawyer the truth.

625 De médico mozo y barbero viejo, cátate.
Beware of the young doctor and the old barber.

Mejor 626 Lo mejor es enemigo de lo bueno.
Best is the enemy of the good.

Mejoría 627 Por mejoría, mi casa dejaría.
Anything for a novelty.

Memoria 628 El mentir pide memoria.
A liar should have a good memory.

629 Más dura la memoria de las injurias recibidas que (la de) los beneficios.
Injuries are written in brass.

Menester 630 Compra lo que no has menester, y venderás lo que no podrás excusar.
Buy what you do not want and you will sell what you cannot spare.

Mentira 631 De una mentira nacen ciento.
One lie makes many.

632　La mentira no tiene pies.
　　　A lie has no legs.

Mentiroso　633　Más presto se coge al mentiroso que al cojo.
　　　The liar is sooner caught than the cripple.

Mercader　634　Mercader que su trato no entienda, cierre la tienda.
　　　A merchant that gains not, loses.

Mercadería　635　El que dice mal de la mercadería, la quiere.
　　　He that speaks ill of the mare would buy her. He that blames would buy.

Mesura　636　En todo conviene mesura.
　　　Moderation in all things.

637　Quien no ha mesura, toda la villa es suya.
　　　He who is without shame, all the world is his.

Miedo　638　Al que mal vive, el miedo le sigue.
　　　A guilty conscience feels continual fear. Who is in fault, suspects everybody.

639　El miedo guarda la viña.
　　　Fear keeps the garden better than the gardener.

640　El miedo pone alas en los pies.
　　　Fear gives wings.

641　Por miedo de gorriones no se dejan de sembrar cañamones.
　　　Forbear not sowing because of birds.

Miel　642　Como miel fue la venida, amarga después la vida.
　　　What is sweet in the mouth is often bitter in the stomach.

643 Haceos (a quien se hace) miel, y os comerán (se lo comen) moscas.
Make yourself all honey and the flies will devour you.

644 No hay miel sin hiel.
Every sweet has its bitter.

645 No se hizo la miel para la boca del asno.
Honey is not for the ass's mouth.

646 Vender miel al colmenero.
Carry coals to Newcastle.

Migaja 647 Vale más una migaja de pan con paz, que toda la casa llena de viandas con rencilla.
A crust of bread in peace is better than a feast in contention.

Mirar 648 Quien adelante no mira, atrás se queda.
He that looks not before, finds himself behind.

Misa 649 No entra en misa la campana, y a todos llama.
Bells call others, but themselves enter not into church.

Mocedad 650 Mocedad ociosa, vejez trabajosa.
An idle youth, a needy age.

Mona 651 Aunque la mona se vista de seda, mona se queda.
An ape is an ape, a varlet is a varlet, though they be clad in silk or scarlet.

Monte 652 No todo el monte es orégano.
There belongs more than whistling to going to plough. There's more to riding than a pair of boots.

Moro	653	No es lo mismo oír decir "moros vienen," que verlos venir. *It is easy to be brave from a safe distance. Who takes a lion when he is absent, fears a mouse present.*
Mosca	654	"Aramos," dijo la mosca al buey. *The fly sat upon the axletree of the chariot-wheel and said," What a dust do I raise!"*
	655	Más moscas se cogen con miel que con hiel. Honey catches more flies than vinegar.
Moza	656	La moza que con viejo se casa, trátese como anciana. A young woman married to an old man must behave like an old woman.
Mozo	657	De mozo, a palacio; de viejo, a beato. *Young devil, old angel.*
	658	El mozo puede morir, y el viejo no puede vivir. Young men may die, old must die.
Mudanza	659	Mudanza de tiempos, bordón de necios. Change of weather is the discourse of fools.
Muela	660	Al que le duele la muela, que se la saque. Better a tooth out than always aching.
	661	Entre dos muelas cordales, nunca metas tus pulgares. *Put not your hand between the bark and the tree.*
Muerte	662	Más vale buena muerte que vida deshonrada. *Better death than dishonour.*
	663	Quien teme la muerte no goza la vida. He that fears death lives not.

Muerto   664   A muertos e idos no hay amigos.
                 To dead men and absent no friends are left.

          665   El muerto al hoyo (la sepultura), y el vivo al bollo
                 (la hogaza).
                 One man's death is another man's bread.

Muestra   666   Por la muestra se conoce el paño.
                 By a sample we may know the whole piece.

Mujer   667   Cuanto más la mujer se mira a la cara, tanto más
                 destruye la casa.
                 The more women look into their glass, the less they
                 look to their house.

          668   La mujer buena, de la casa vacía hace llena.
                 Men build houses, women build homes.

          669   La mujer del ciego, ¿para quién se afeita?
                 The blind man's wife needs no painting.

          670   La mujer dice y hace cuanto le place.
                 Women will have their wills.

          671   La mujer placera dice de todos, y todos de ella.
                 A gossip speaks ill of all and all of her.

          672   La mujer ríe cuando puede y llora cuando quiere.
                 A woman laughs when she can but cries whenever
                 she wishes.

          673   La mujer y el vidrio siempre están en peligro.
                 A woman and glass are ever in danger.

          674   La mujer y la tela (cibera), no la cates a la candela.
                 Choose neither a woman nor linen by candlelight.

          675   Mujer, viento y fortuna (ventura), pronto se
                 mudan.
                 Women are as wavering as the wind.

          676   Tres mujeres y un ganso hacen un mercado.
                 Three women and a goose make a market.

Mula	677	Quien quisiera mula sin tacha, ándese a pata. He who wants a mule without fault, must walk on foot.
Mundo	678	Cuando amanece, para todo el mundo amanece. *The sun shines upon all alike.*
	679	Este mundo es golfo redondo; quien no sabe nadar vase al hondo. *The world is a ladder for some to go up and some down.*

N

Nacer	680	Al nacer, empezamos a morir. As soon as a man is born, he begins to die.
	681	No con quien naces, sino con quien paces. *Nurture is above (passes) nature.*
Nada	682	De nada no se hace nada. Nothing comes of (from) nothing.
Nadador	683	El mejor nadador se ahoga (es del agua). Good swimmers at length are drowned. *The best drivers have wrecks.*
Naranja	684	No se ha de exprimir tanto la naranja que amargue el zumo. *The orange that is squeezed too hard yields a bitter juice.*
Necesidad	685	De la necesidad nace el consejo. *Necessity is the mother of invention.*
	686	La necesidad carece de ley. Necessity knows no law.
	687	La necesidad hace a la vieja trotar (mucho). Need makes the old wife trot.

688   La necesidad hace maestro.
      Poverty is the mother of all arts.

Necio   689   A cada necio agrada su porrada.
                  Every ass likes to hear himself bray.

690   Cuando el necio es acordado, el mercado es ya
      pasado.
      *When the fool has made up his mind, the market
      has gone by.*

691   El necio hace al fin lo que el discreto al principio.
      *What a fool does in the end, the wise man does at
      the beginning.*

692   Más vale ser necio que porfiado.
      Better a fool than a knave.

693   Muchas veces el necio dice un buen consejo.
      A fool may give a wise man counsel.

Negro   694   Sobre negro no hay tintura.
                  Black takes no other hue.

Nido   695   En los nidos de antaño no hay pájaros hogaño.
                 There are no birds in last year's nests.

Niño   696   De niño y de loco, todos tenemos un poco.
                 *Men are but children of a larger growth. We have all
                 been fools once in our lives.*

697   Dicen los niños en el solejar lo que oyen a sus pa-
      dres en el hogar.
      Little children have big ears.

698   Los niños y los locos dicen la(s) verdad(es).
      Children and fools speak the truth.

Noche	699	De noche todos los gatos son pardos. All cats are black (grey) at night.
	700	La noche es capa de pecadores. *He that does ill, hates the light. Darkness has no shame.*
	701	Lo que la noche se hace, a la mañana parece. What is done in the night, appears in the day.
Noticia	702	Sin noticias, buenas noticias. No news is good news.
Nuevo	703	Todo lo nuevo agrada. Everything new is fine.
	704	Nada hay nuevo bajo el sol. There's nothing new under the sun.
Nudo	705	A mal nudo, mal cuño. Knotty timber must have sharp wedges.

O

Oblada	706	Quien lleva las obladas, que taña las campanas. *Those who take the profits should also bear the expense.*
Obligación	707	Primero es la obligación que la devoción. *Business before pleasure.*
Obra	708	La obra es la que alaba al maestro. The work praises the workman.
	709	Obra del común, obra de ningún. *Everybody's business is nobody's business.*
	710	Obra empezada, medio acabada. *Well begun is half done.*
	711	Obras son amores, que no buenas razones. *Good words without deeds are rushes and reeds.*
Obsequio	712	Desconfía de los obsequios de tu enemigo. *Gifts from enemies are dangerous.*
Ocasión	713	La ocasión hace al ladrón. Opportunity makes the thief.
Ociosidad	714	La ociosidad es madre de (todos) los vicios. *Idleness is the root of all evil.*

Oficio 715 Quien ha oficio, ha beneficio.
A handful of trade is a handful of gold.

Ojo 716 El ojo del amo engorda el caballo.
The master's eye makes the horse fat.

717 Lejos de ojos, lejos del corazón.
Out of sight, out of mind.

718 Lo que ve el ojo, cree el corazón.
What the eyes see, the heart believes.

719 Los ojos son el espejo del alma.
The eyes are the mirror (window) of the soul.

720 Más ven cuatro ojos que dos.
Four eyes see more than two.

721 Ojos que no ven, corazón que no llora (siente).
What the eye doesn't see, the heart doesn't grieve
for.

Olla 722 A la olla que hierve, ninguna mosca se atreve.
Flies never bother a boiling pot.

723 No hay olla tan fea, que no tenga su cobertera.
Every pot has its cover.

724 Olla de muchos, mal mejida y peor cocida.
A pot that belongs to many is ill-stirred and worse
boiled.

Ollero 725 Cada ollero alaba su puchero.
Every cook praises his own broth (stew).

Oración 726 La oración breve sube al cielo.
A short prayer penetrates heaven.

727 Oración de perro no va al cielo.
The prayers of the wicked won't prevail.

Oro   728   Donde el oro habla, la lengua calla.
                  When gold speaks, other tongues are dumb.

            729   No es oro todo lo que reluce.
                  All that glitters is not gold.

Oveja   730   A ruin oveja la lana le pesa.
                  A lazy sheep thinks its wool heavy.

            731   Cada oveja con su pareja.
                  Every sheep with its like. *Birds of a feather flock to-
                  gether.*

            732   Hazte oveja y te comerán los lobos.
                  Make yourself a sheep and the wolves will eat you.

            733   Oveja que bala, bocado pierde.
                  The sheep that bleats loses a mouthful.

            734   Ovejas bobas, por do va una van todas.
                  One sheep follows another.

P

Paciencia	735	Con la paciencia se gana el cielo (todo se logra). *Patient men win the day. They that have patience may accomplish anything.*
	736	Paciencia muchas veces ofendida, trastorna el juicio. *Patience provoked turns to fury.*
Padre	737	A padre endurador (guardador), hijo gastador. A miser's son is a spendthrift.
	738	De padre santo, hijo diablo. *Many a good father has a bad son.*
	739	Entre padres y hermanos no metas tus manos. *Put not your hand between the bark and the tree.*
	740	Quien (el) padre tiene alcalde, seguro va a juicio. *He whose father is judge goes safe to his trial.*
	741	Un padre para cien hijos, y no cien hijos para un padre. *One father is enough to govern one hundred sons, but not a hundred sons one father.*
Paga	742	Paga adelantada, paga viciosa. Payment in advance is evil payment.

Pagador   743   Al buen pagador no le duelen prendas.
A good paymaster needs no surety.

Paja   744   Ver la paja en el ojo ajeno, y no la viga en el
nuestro.
*You can see a mote in another's eye but cannot see a
beam in your own.*

Pájaro   745   A cada pajarillo gusta su nidillo.
Every bird likes its own nest best.

746   A chico pajarillo, chico nidillo.
Little bird, little nest.

747   Cada pajarito tiene su higadito.
No viper so little but has its venom.

748   Cada pájaro canta su canción.
Everyone speaks for his own interest.

749   Más vale pájaro en mano que ciento (buitre) vo-
lando.
A bird in the hand is worth two in the bush.

750   Pájaro mal nacido es el que ensucia su nido.
It is an ill bird that fouls its own nest.

751   Pájaro viejo no entra en jaula.
*You cannot catch old birds with chaff. An old fox is
not easily snared.*

Palabra   752   La palabra de la boca, mucho vale y poco cuesta.
Pleasant words are valued and do not cost much.

753   Las palabras son femeninas, y los hechos son
machos.
Deeds are masculine, words are feminine.

754   Más hiere mala palabra que espada afilada.
Words cut (hurt) more than swords.

755   Palabra y piedra suelta no tiene vuelta.
A word and a stone let go cannot be called back.

756   Palabras de santo, uñas de gato.
A honey tongue, a heart of gall.

757   Palabras y plumas el viento las lleva (tumba).
Words and feathers the wind carries away.

758   Pocas palabras cumplen al buen entendedor.
Few words to the wise suffice.

Palo   759   De tal palo, tal astilla.
A chip off the old block. As the old cock crows, the young cock learns.

Pan   760   A pan duro, diente agudo.
An old horse for a hard road.

761   Aquél loar debemos, cuyo pan comemos.
Whose bread I eat, his song I sing.

762   Ara bien y hondo, y cogerás pan en abondo.
Plough deep and you will have plenty of corn.

763   Más vale pan con amor que gallina con dolor.
Dry bread with love is better than fried chicken with fear and trembling.

764   Mejor es pan duro que ninguno.
A crust is better than no bread.

765   No hay para pan, y compraremos musco.
Silks and satins put out the fire in the chimney.

766   No sólo de pan vive el hombre.
Man does not live on bread alone.

767   Pan ajeno, caro cuesta.
Bitter is the bread of charity.

768 Quien da pan a perro ajeno, pierde el pan y pierde el perro.
He that keeps another man's dog shall have nothing left him but the line.

Paño 769 No hay paño sin raza.
The best cloth may have a moth in it.

Par 770 A la par es negar y tarde dar.
To refuse and give tardily is all the same.

Paranza 771 Bien saben las paranzas quién pasó por las losas.
He knows how many beans make five.

Pardal 772 A todo pardal viejo no lo toman en todas redes.
You cannot catch old birds with chaff.

Pastor 773 El buen pastor esquila las ovejas, pero no las despelleja.
It is the part of a good shepherd to shear the flock, not flay it.

Pato 774 Pato, ganso y ansarón, tres cosas suenan y una son.
Goose, gander and gosling are three sounds but one thing.

Patria 775 Donde está uno bien, allí está la patria.
Where it is well with me, there is my country.

Paz 776 Si quieres asegurar la paz, prepárate para la guerra.
If you desire peace, prepare for war.

Pecado 777 Pecado confesado (encelado) es medio perdonado.
A sin confessed (that is hidden) is half-forgiven.

Pecar	778	Humano es pecar, diabólico perseverar. *To err is human, to persist in it, beastly.*
Pedir	779	Pedir sobrado por salir mediado. *Ask much to have little.*
	780	Quien no sabe pedir, no sabe vivir. He that cannot ask, cannot live.
	781	Quien pide no escoge. *Beggars can't be choosers.*
Pedro	782	Algo va de Pedro a Pedro. There is some difference between Peter and Peter.
Pelea	783	De pequeña pelea nace muy gran rencor. *From one quarrel come a hundred sins. The pain of dispute exceeds by far its utility.*
Peligro	784	En el peligro se conoce al amigo. *Adversity is the touchstone of friendship.*
	785	Nunca un peligro sin otro se vence. *Dangers are conquered by dangers.*
	786	Quien ama el peligro, en él perece. He that loves danger shall perish therein.
Pelo	787	Aunque muda el pelo la raposa, su natural no despoja. The fox changes his skin but not his habits.
Peña	788	Allégate a la peña, mas no te despeña. *Mind other men, but most yourself.*
Pera	789	Quien dice mal de la pera, ése la lleva. *He that will slight my horse will buy my horse.*

Perder	790	Lo que con unos se pierde, con otros se gana. *What we lose in hake, we shall have in herring.*
	791	Más vale perder que más perder. *Better a mischief than an inconvenience. Lose a leg rather than a life.*
Pereza	792	La pereza es llave de pobredad. *Idleness is the key of beggary.*
Perro	793	A perro malo, correa corta. *A mischievous dog must be tied short.*
	794	A perro viejo, nunca cuz cuz (tus tus). *No playing with straw before an old cat.*
	795	El perro con rabia, de su amo traba. *The mad dog bites his master.*
	796	El perro de herrero duerme a las martilladas y despierta a las dentelladas. *Like the smith's dog that sleeps at the noise of a hammer and wakes at the crunching of teeth.*
	797	El perro del hortelano, que no come las berzas ni las deja comer al amo. *Like the gardener's dog that neither eats cabbages himself, nor lets anybody else.*
	798	El perro flaco todo es pulgas. *The lean dog is all fleas.*
	799	El perro roe el hueso porque no puede tragárselo. *Dogs gnaw bones because they cannot swallow them.*
	800	El perro viejo no ladra a tocón. *An old dog barks not in vain.*
	801	Muerto el perro, se acabó la rabia. *A dead dog cannot bite.*

802   No hay que despertar al perro que duerme.
       Let sleeping dogs lie.

803   Perrillo de muchas bodas, no come en ninguna
       por comer en todas.
       Dogs that put up many hares kill none.

804   Perro ladrador, poco mordedor.
       A barking dog never bites.

805   Quien con perros se echa, con pulgas se levanta.
       If you lie down with dogs, you'll get up with fleas.

Pez (el)   806   El pez grande se traga al chico.
               The big fish eat the little ones.

807   El pez que busca el anzuelo, busca su duelo.
       The fish will soon be caught that nibbles at every
       bait.

Pez (la)   808   Quien anda con pez, se manchará los dedos.
               He that deals in dirt has foul fingers.

Pie   809   El pie del dueño, estiércol es para la heredad.
                  The master's footsteps fatten the soil, and his foot the
                  ground.

810   No hay que buscar tres pies al gato.
       Don't expect three legs on a cat when you know he
       has four.

Piedra   811   Piedra movediza, nunca moho la cobija.
                     †*A rolling stone gathers no moss.*

812   Piedra sin agua, no aguza en la fragua.
       Mills will not grind if you give them not water.

Piel   813   No se debe vender la piel antes de matar el oso.
                   Don't sell the skin before you have caught the bear.

Pierna	814	No extiendas la pierna más de lo que alcanza la manta (sábana). Stretch your legs according to your coverlet. *Don't stretch out your arm farther than the sleeve will reach.*
Placer	815	Los placeres son por onzas y los males por arrobas. *Short pleasure, long lament.*
Planta	816	Planta muchas veces traspuesta, ni crece ni medra. *A tree often transplanted neither grows nor thrives.*
Plazo	817	No hay plazo que no llegue, ni deuda que no se pague. *Punishment comes slowly, but it comes. Every sin carries its own punishment.*
Pobre	818	Cuando pobre, franca; cuando rica, avarienta. *Poor and liberal, rich and covetous.*
	819	No los que tienen poco son pobres, mas los que mucho desean. He is not poor that has little, but he that desires much.
Pobreza	820	La pobreza hace comer sin guisar. *Poor folks are glad of porridge.*
	821	Ni te abatas por pobreza, ni te ensalces por riqueza. *It is harder to be poor without murmuring than to be rich without arrogance.*
	822	Pobreza no es vileza. Poverty is no disgrace.
	823	Quien pobreza tien, de sus deudos es desdén, y el rico, de serlo, de todos es deudo. *The poor is hated even of his neighbours, but the rich have many friends.*

Poco	824	De lo poco, poco, y de lo mucho, nada. *The higher the hill, the lower the grass. Generosity is more charitable than wealth.*
	825	Lo poco agrada, y lo mucho enfada. *A little wind kindles, much puts out the fire.*
	826	Muchos pocos hacen un mucho (algo). Many smalls make a great. *A little makes a lot.*
Poder	827	Quien cuando puede no quiere, bien es que cuando quiera no pueda. He who would not when he could, is not able when he would.
	828	Si no puedes lo que quieres, quiere lo que puedes. *Since we cannot get what we want, let us like what we can get.*
Porfía	829	Porfía mata la caza. Perseverance kills the game.
Posada	830	El salir de la posada es la mayor jornada. *The hardest step is over the threshold.*
Postrero	831	El postrero que sabe las desgracias es el marido. *The husband is always the last to know.*
Potro	832	De potro sarnoso, caballo hermoso. Ragged colts make fine horses.
Predicar	833	Bien predica quien bien vive. He preaches well who lives well.
Pregunta	834	No toda pregunta merece respuesta. Not every question deserves an answer.

Preguntar 835 Quien pregunta, no yerra.
It is better to ask twice than to go wrong once.

Preso 836 Preso por mil, preso por mil y quinientos.
In for a penny, in for a pound.

Prevenir 837 Más vale prevenir que ser prevenidos.
Prevent rather than repent.

Principio 838 De pequeños principios resultan grandes fines.
From small beginnings come great things.

839 Principio quieren las cosas.
Everything must have a beginning.

Prisa 840 A gran prisa, gran vagar.
More haste (hurry), less speed. The man in a hurry is in a hurry to go nowhere.

841 Date prisa lentamente.
Make haste slowly.

Procesión 842 No se puede repicar y andar en la procesión.
No man can sup and blow together.

Profeta 843 Nadie es profeta en su tierra.
No man is a prophet in his own country.

Prometer 844 Quien mucho promete, poco da.
A long tongue is a sign of a short hand.

845 Quien promete, en deuda se mete.
A promise is a debt.

846 Una cosa es prometer, y otra es lo prometido mantener.
It is one thing to promise, another to perform.

| Propósito | 847 | El propósito muda el sabio, el necio persevera. |
| | | A wise man changes his mind, a fool never does. |

847 El propósito muda el sabio, el necio persevera.
A wise man changes his mind, a fool never does.

848 Quien sus propósitos parla, no se casa.
Tell everybody your business and the devil will do it for you.

Pronto

849 Pronto y bien nunca van juntos.
Good and quickly seldom meet.

Prueba

850 Por la prueba se conoce al amigo.
Adversity is the touchstone (test) of friendship.

Puerco

851 A cada puerco le llega su San Martín.
Every hog has his Martinmas.

852 Al más ruin puerco, la mejor bellota.
The worst hog gets the best pear.

853 El puerco sarnoso revuelve la pocilga.
The leanest pig squeals the most.

Puerta

854 Cierra tu puerta y loa tus vecinos.
Lock your door and keep your neighbours honest.

855 Cuando una puerta se cierra, otra (ciento) se abre(n).
When one door closes, another one opens.

856 Puerta abierta, al santo tienta.
An open door may tempt a saint.

Pulga

857 Cada uno tiene su modo de matar pulgas.
Every man in his own way.

Pupa

858 Entre pupa y burujón, Dios escoja lo mejor. *Where bad's the best, bad must be the choice.*

Q

Queja   859   Más vale buena queja que mala paga.
                     Better to be a good loser than a poor winner.

Querer   860   A quien lo quiere celeste, que le cueste.
                     Everything that is worth having must be paid for.

               861   Cuando uno no quiere, dos no barajan.
                     When one will not, two cannot quarrel.
                     It takes two to make a quarrel.

               862   Do no te quieren mucho, no vayas a menudo.
                     Where men are well used, they'll frequent there.

               863   Querer es poder.
                     Where there's a will, there's a way.

               864   Quien bien quiere, tarde olvida.
                     He who loves well will never forget.

               865   Quien bien te quiere, te hará llorar.
                     *You always hurt the one you love. He who loves well,
                     chastises well.*

               866   Quien todo lo quiere, todo lo pierde.
                     All covet, all lose.

               867   Si no como queremos, pasamos como podemos.
                     He that may not do as he would must do as he may.

               868   Si quieres ser bien servido, sírvete a ti mismo.
                     If you would be well served, serve yourself.

869   Si quieres vivir sano, hazte viejo temprano.
An old young man will be a young old man. Old young and old long.

R

Rabo   870   De rabo de puerco, nunca buen virote.
You can't make a silk purse out of a sow's ear.

Ramera   871   A la ramera y al juglar, a la vejez les viene el mal.
Every dissipation of youth has to be paid for with a draft on old age.

Raposo   872   A raposo durmiente, no le amanece la gallina en el vientre.
The sleeping fox catches no poultry. The sleepy fox has seldom feathered breakfasts.

               873   Cada raposo guarde su cola.
Physician, heal thyself. Self do, self have.

Rato   874   Más vale rato acucioso que día perezoso.
Better to live like a lion for a day than to live like a lamb for a hundred years. A little along is better than a long none.

Ratón   875   Acogí al ratón en mi agujero, y volvióseme heredero.
Nourish a snake in one's bosom.

               876   Ratón que no sabe más que un horado, presto es cazado.
The mouse that has but one hole is soon caught.

| **Razón** | 877 | La razón no quiere fuerza. |
| | | *Those who are right need not talk loudly.* |

| **Regla** | 878 | No hay regla sin excepción. |
| | | There's no rule without an exception. |

| **Reír** | 879 | Ríe bien el que ríe último. |
| | | He who laughs last laughs best. |

Remedio	880	Con mala persona, el remedio - mucha tierra en medio.
		The best remedy against an ill man is much ground between.
	881	A todo hay remedio, sino a la muerte.
		There is a remedy for all things but death.
	882	A veces es peor el remedio que la enfermedad.
		Sometimes the remedy is worse than the disease.

Remiendo	883	No hay mejor remiendo que el del mismo paño.
		The best patch is of the same cloth.
	884	Nunca falta un remiendo (roto) para un descosido.
		Scabby donkeys scent each other over nine hills.
		There isn't a pot too crooked but there's a lid to fit it.

Rey	885	A rey muerto, rey puesto.
		The king is dead, long live the king!
	886	Cual es el rey, tal la grey.
		Like priest, like people.
	887	Donde está el rey, está la corte.
		Where the king is, there is the court.
	888	Nuevo rey, nueva ley.
		New lords, new laws.

Rico	889	No es rico el que más ha, mas el que menos codicia. *He is not rich that possesses much, but he that is content with what he has.*
Río	890	A río revuelto, ganancia de pescadores. *It is good fishing in troubled waters.*
	891	Donde va más hondo el río, hace menos ruido. *When a river does not make any noise, it is either empty or very full.*
Risa	892	De la risa al duelo, un pelo. *Laugh before breakfast, cry before sunset.*
Rodilla	893	La rodilla de Mari García, que más me ensucia que me limpia. *A bad broom leaves a dirty room.*
Roma	894	Cuando a Roma (por donde) fueres, haz como vieres. When in Rome, do as the Romans.
	895	Hablando de Roma, el burro se asoma. *Talk of the devil and he is sure to appear.*
	896	Por todas partes se va a Roma. All roads lead to Rome.
Romper	897	El que rompe (los vasos), (los) paga. *The deed comes back upon the doer.*
Ropa	898	La ropa sucia se debe lavar en casa. *Don't wash your dirty linen in public.*
Rosa	899	No hay rosa sin espinas. No rose without thorns.

Rosario	900	El rosario al cuello, y el diablo en el cuerpo. *The cross on the breast and the devil in the heart.*
Ruego	901	Más vale el ruego del amigo que el hierro del enemigo. *Power itself has not one-half the might of gentleness.*
Ruin	902	Al ruin, cuando lo mientan, luego viene. *Speak of the devil and he's sure to appear.*
	903	Al ruin, ruin y medio. *Set a thief to catch a thief.*
	904	Ruin sea quien por ruin se tiene. *If you don't think well of yourself, no one else will.* *Evil to him who evil thinks.*
	905	Un ruin ido, otro venido. *Ill comes often on the back of worse. Trouble never comes singly.*

S

Saber	906	El que nada sabe, de nada duda. He that knows nothing doubts nothing. *He who doubts nothing, knows nothing.*
	907	El saber no ocupa lugar. *Knowledge is no burden.*
	908	Saber es poder. *Knowledge is power.*
Salsa	909	Vale (cuesta) más la salsa (el salmorejo) que los perdigones (el conejo). *The game is not worth the candle.*
Salvo	910	En salvo está el que repica. *It is easy to be brave from a safe distance.*
Salto	911	A gran salto, gran quebranto. *Hasty climbers have sudden falls.*
Sancho	912	Al buen callar llaman Sancho (santo). *He who knows how to be silent knows a great deal.*
	913	Con lo que Sancho sana, Domingo adolece. *One man's meat is another man's poison.*

Sangre	914	La sangre se hereda y el vicio se apega.
		Blood is inherited and virtue is acquired.
Santo	915	Desnudar un santo para vestir otro.
		Rob Peter to pay Paul.
	916	Rogar al santo hasta pasar el charco (tranco).
		The river past and God forgotten.
Sardina	917	Con una sardina pescar una trucha.
		Throw out a sprat to catch a mackerel.
Sartén	918	Dijo la sartén a la caldera: quítate allá, culinegra (tiznera).
		The pot calls the kettle black.
	919	Saltar de la sartén y dar en las brasas.
		Jump from the frying pan into the fire.
Sayo	920	Debajo del buen sayo está el hombre malo.
		Under a good cloak may be a bad man.
	921	Remienda tu sayo (paño) y pasarás tu año.
		A stitch in time saves nine.
Secreto	922	A quien dices el secreto, das tu libertad.
		To whom you reveal your secrets you yield your liberty.
		He that tells a secret is another's servant.
	923	Secreto de dos, sábelo Dios; secreto de tres, toda res.
		It is no secret that is known to three.
Sembrar	924	Como siembras, cogerás.
		As you sow, you shall reap.

925   Siembra quien habla y recoge quien calla.
He that speaks sows, and he that holds his peace gathers.

Sendero   926   Cada sendero tiene su atolladero.
There was never a good town but had a mire at the end of it.

Señor   927   A escaso señor, artero servidor.
A bad master makes a bad servant.

928   A tal señor, tal honor.
Such answer as man gives, such will he get. Honour will honour meet. Honour to whom honour is due.

Ser   929   Lo que fuere, sonará.
The event proves the act.

Servir   930   Quien sirve a muchos, no sirve a ninguno.
If you help everybody you help nobody.
A friend to everybody is a friend to nobody.

Seso   931   Quien poco seso ha, aína lo expiende.
A fool's bolt is soon shot.

Sevilla   932   Quien fue a Sevilla perdió su silla.
If you leave your place, you lose it.

Sol   933   Cuando el sol sale, para todos sale.
The sun shines upon all alike.

934   Sol que mucho madruga, poco dura.
Soon ripe, soon rotten.

Solo   935   Más vale solo que mal acompañado.
Better alone than in bad company.

Solomo 936 Cuando no tengo solomo, de todo como.
If you have not a capon, feed on an onion.

Soplar 937 Soplar y sorber no puede junto ser.
No man can sup and blow together.

Sordo 938 No hay peor sordo que el que no quiere oír.
There is none so deaf as those who will not hear.

Subida 939 Cuanto mayor es la subida, tanto mayor es la
descendida.
The higher the mountain, the greater the descent.
The higher standing, the lower fall.

Suegra 940 No se acuerda la suegra que fue nuera.
The mother-in-law remembers not that she was a
daughter-in-law.

T

Tardanza	941	Buena es la tardanza que hace la carrera segura. *That delay is good which makes the way the safer.*
Tarde	942	Más vale tarde que nunca. *Better late than never.*
Tejado	943	Quien tiene tejado de vidrio, no tire piedras al de su vecino. *People who live in glass houses shouldn't throw stones.*
Tener	944	Quien más tiene, más quiere. *The more you have, the more you want.* *Much would have more.*
Tiempo	945	A su (con el) tiempo maduran las brevas (uvas). *Time and straw make medlars ripe.*
	946	Cual el tiempo, tal el tiento. *New circumstances, new controls.*
	947	Nunca «tiempo hay» hizo cosa buena. *"Time enough" lost the ducks.*
	948	Quien en tiempo huye, en tiempo acude. *He that fights and runs away may live to fight another day.*

949   Quien quisiere ser mucho tiempo viejo,
       comiéncelo presto.
       He that would be old long, must be old betimes
       (early).

950   Vuela el tiempo como el viento.
       Time flies like the wind.

Tierra   951   En cada tierra su uso, y en cada casa su costumbre.
                     *So many countries, so many customs. Every country
                     has its own customs.*

              952   En tierra de ciegos, el tuerto es rey.
                     In the country of the blind, the one-eyed man is
                     king.

Toca   953   Dos tocas en un hogar, mal se pueden concertar.
                     Two women in the same house can never agree.

Tomar   954   Más vale un «toma» que dos «te daré.»
                     Better is one "Accipe" than twice to say "Dabo tibi."

Tonel   955   Los toneles vacíos son los que hacen más ruido.
                     Empty barrels make the most noise.

Tonto   956   No hay tonto para su provecho.
                     A man is a lion in his own cause.

Toro   957   Pelean los toros, y mal para las ramas.
                     *The pleasures of the mighty are the tears of the poor.
                     The humble suffer from the folly of the great.*

Trabajo   958   Cual el trabajo, tal la paga.
                     A workman is worthy of his hire.

Traición	959	La traición aplace, mas no el que la hace.
		We love the treason but hate the traitor.
Trigo	960	No es lo mismo predicar que dar trigo.
		An ounce of practice is worth a pound of precept.
Tripa	961	Tripas llevan corazón, que no corazón tripas.
		The belly carries the legs. A full belly makes a brave heart.
Trompeta	962	Morir ahorcados, o comer con trompetas.
		Either win the saddle or lose the horse.

U

Uno	963	Uno y ninguno, todo es uno.
		One and none is all one.
Uña	964	Por la uña se conoce al león.
		The lion is known by his claws.
Usar	965	Lo que se usa no se excusa.
		Once a use ever and ever a custom.
Uso	966	El uso hace maestro.
		Use makes mastery.

V

Vaca 967 Más vale(n) vaca (cardos) en paz, que pollos con agraz.
A crust of bread in peace is better than a feast in contention. Dry bread with love is better than fried chicken with fear and trembling.

968 Quien come la vaca del rey, a cien años paga los huesos.
He that eats the king's goose shall be choked by the feathers.

Valer 969 Tanto vales cuanto tienes.
A man's worth is the worth of his land.

Vaquero 970 Ayer vaquero y hoy caballero.
The king can make a knight, but not a gentleman.

Vaquilla 971 Cuando te dieren la vaquilla, acude con la soguilla.
Take while the taking's good.

Varón 972 Al buen varón, tierras ajenas su patria le son.
A wise man esteems every place to be his own country.

Vasija 973 A la vasija nueva dura el resabio de lo que se echó en ella.
The cask savours of the first fill.

Vejez	974	La vejez es un hospital donde caben todas las enfermedades. Old age is a hospital that takes in all diseases.
Vencida	975	A las tres va la vencida. The third time's lucky. *All things thrive at thrice.* *Three strikes and you're out.*
Vendimia	976	Después de vendimias, cuévanos. Baskets after vintage.
Ventura	977	Viene ventura a quien la procura. *Every man is the architect of his own fortune.*
Verdad	978	El lenguaje de la verdad es sencillo. The expression of truth is simplicity.
Vergüenza	979	Quien no tiene vergüenza, toda la calle es suya. *He who is without shame, all the world is his.*
Vía	980	A luengas vías, luengas mentiras. *A traveller may lie with authority.*
Vicente	981	¿Dónde va Vicente? Donde va la gente. *One sheep follows another. Monkey see, monkey do.*
Victoria	982	No se debe cantar victoria hasta después de haber vencido. Don't sing your triumph before you have conquered. *Triumph not before the victory.*
Vid	983	De buena vid planta la viña, y de buena madre la hija. Take a vine of a good soil, and the daughter of a good mother.

| Vida | 984 | Mientras hay vida, hay esperanza. |
| | | While there's life, there's hope. |

| | 985 | Vida sin amigo, muerte sin testigo. |
| | | Life without a friend is death without a witness. |

| Viejo | 986 | No le quiere mal quien le hurta al viejo lo que ha de cenar. |
| | | He wrongs not an old man that steals his supper from him. |

| Viento | 987 | Quien siembra vientos, recoge tempestades. |
| | | He who sows the wind reaps the whirlwind. |

| Vientre | 988 | El vientre ayuno no oye (a) ninguno. |
| | | A hungry belly has no ears. |

| Villa | 989 | Quien ruin es en su villa, ruin será en Sevilla. |
| | | *Who goes a beast to Rome, a beast returns.* |

Villano	990	Al villano dale el pie, y se tomará la mano.
		Give him (a fool) a finger and he'll take a hand.
		Give a fool an inch and he'll take a yard (mile).

| Vino | 991 | El buen vino no ha menester pregonero. |
| | | Good wine needs no bush. |

| | 992 | En el mejor vino hay heces. |
| | | *No silver without its dross. No garden without its weeds. The best cloth may have a moth in it.* |

| | 993 | En el vino está la verdad. |
| | | In wine there is truth. |

| Vivir | 994 | Como se vive, se muere. |
| | | Such a life, such a death. |

995   Vivir y dejar vivir.
Live and let live.

Y

Yegua   996   El que desecha la yegua, ése la lleva.
He that will slight my horse, will buy my horse.

Z

Zamora	997	No se ganó Zamora en una hora.
		Rome wasn't built in a day.
Zapato	998	Cada uno sabe dónde le aprieta el zapato.
		Everyone knows where his shoe pinches.
Zapatero	999	Zapatero, a tus zapatos.
		Let the cobbler stick to his last.
Zorra	1000	Mucho sabe la zorra, pero más quien la toma.
		The fox knows much, but more he that catches him.

Bibliography

Abrahams, Roger D. and Babcock, Barbara A. "The Literary Use of Proverbs." *Journal of American Folklore.* 90 (1977), 414-429.

Acuña, Luis Alberto. "Catalogación del material paremiológico." *Revista de folklore* (Bogotá, Colombia), no.4 (1949), 1-11.

Alarcos Llorach, E. "La lengua de los «Proverbios Morales» de don Sem Tob." *Revista de filología española,* 35 (1951), 249-309.

Alonso Hernández, José Luis. "Parémiologie et critique socio-historique: quelques remarques sur le «Teatro universal de proverbios» de Sebastián de Horozco." *Espace, idéologie et société au XVIème siècle.* Ed. Hernández, Brunet, Plaisance and Quilliet. Grenoble: Presses Universitaires, 1975, 13-34.

Amador de los Ríos, Don José. "Ilustración sobre los refranes, considerados como elemento del arte." in id. *Historia critica de la literatura española.* Madrid: José Rodríguez, 1862. II, 503-538.

Amaya Valencia, Eduardo. "Problemas de paremiología." *Revista de folklore* (Bogota, Colombia), no.2 (1947), 107-111.

Arora, Shirley L. "El que nace para tamal...: A Study in Proverb Patterning." *Folklore Americas,* 28 (1968), 55-79.

_____ "The «El que nace» Proverbs: A Supplement." *Journal of American Lore,* 1 (1975), 185-198.

Benas, Baron Louis. "On the Proverbs of European Nations." *Proceedings of the Literary and Philosophical Society of Liverpool,* no.32 (1877-78), 291-332.

Brandes, Stanley H. "The Selection Process in Proverb Use: A Spanish Example." *Southern Folklore Quarterly,* 38(1974), 167-186.

Campos, J.G. and Barella, A. *Diccionario de Refranes.* Espasa Calpe: Madrid, 1993.

Cannobio, Augustín G. *Refranes chilenos.* Santiago de Chile, 1901.

Casares, Julio. "La frase proverbial y el refrán." *Universidad Pontificia Bolivariana,* 27 (1964), 36-49.

Casey, Guillermo. *Intérprete anglo-hispano.* Barcelona, 1836.

Cazaurang, Jean-Jacques. "Eléments de parémiologie comparée: proverbes espagnols et béarnais." *Bulletin philologique et historique,* 1 (1972), 43-64.

Coll y Vehí, José. *Los refranes del Quijote.* Barcelona, 1876.

Collins, John. *A Dictionary of Spanish Proverbs Compiled from the Best Authorities in the Spanish Language, Translated into English.* London, 1823.

Combert, Louis. *Recherche sur le "refranero" castillan.* Paris: Société d'édition "Les Belles Lettres," 1971.

Correas, Gonzalo. *Vocabulario de refranes y frases proverbiales.* Madrid, 1924.

De Barros, Alonso. *Proverbios morales.* Baeza, 1615.

De Garay, Blasco. *Dos cartas en refranes.* Toledo, 1541.

De Horozco, Sebastián. *Recopilación de refranes y adagios.* Madrid, 1599.

De Valles, Pedro. *Libro de refranes.* Toledo, 1549.

ed. Editorial Sintes. *Diccionario de Aforismos, Proverbios, y Refranes.* 4a. edición. Barcelona, 1967.

ed. Editorial de Vecchi. *El libro de refranes.* Barcelona, 1994.

Ernouf, Anita Bonilla. *Proverbs and Proverbial Phrases in the "Celestina."* Diss. Columbia University, 1970.

Galloway, Clifford H. *Spanish Proverbs, Sayings, Idioms, and Random Selections with their English Translation.* New York: Spanish-American Printing Company, 1944.

Gómez-Tabanera, José Manuel. "El refranero español." *El Folklore Español.* Ed. Gómez-Tabanera, J.M. Madrid: Instituto Español de Antropologia aplicada. 1968. 389-431.

Haller, José. *Altspanische Sprichwörter und sprichwörtliche Redensarten.* Regensburg, 1883.

Jente, Richard. "A Review of Proverb Literature Since 1920." *Corona. Studies in Celebration of the Eightieth Birthday of Samuel Singer.* Eds. Schirokauer, A. and Paulsen, W. Durham: Duke University Press, 1941. 23-44.

_____ "El refrán." *Folklore Americas,* 7, nos. 1-2 (1947), 1-11.

Kleiser, Luis Martínez. *Refranero general ideológico español.* Madrid, 1953.

Leval, Ramón A. *Paremiología chilena.* Santiago de Chile: Imprenta Universitaria, 1928.

López de Mendoza, D. Iñigo (Marqués de Santillana). *Refranes que dicen las viejas tras el fuego.* Sevilla, 1512.

Marín, Francisco Rodríguez. *Más de 21.000 refranes castellanos.* Madrid, 1926.

_____ *Doce mil seiscientos refranes más.* Madrid, 1930

Mieder, Wolfgang. "Hilfsquellen für Sprichwörterübersetzungen." *Sprachspiegel.* 33 (1977), 56-57.

_____ *International Proverb Scholarship, An Annotated Bibliography.* New York: Garland, 1982.

_____, Kingsbury S.A., Harder K.B. *A Dictionary of American Proverbs.* Oxford:OUP, 1992.

Mombert, Isidor J. "A Chapter on Proverbs." *Bibliotheca Sacra,* 28 (1881), 593-621.

Moya, Ismael. *Refranero. Refranes, proverbios, adagios, frases proverbiales, modismos refranescos, giros y otras formas paremiológicas tradicionales en la República Argentina.* Buenos Aires: Imprenta de la Universidad, 1944.

Murciego, Pablo León. *Los refranes filosóficos castellanos.* Zaragoza, 1962.

Nin y Tudó. *Para la mujer.* Barcelona, 1881.

O'Kane, Eleanor S. "What's in a Name?" *Proverbium,* 15 (1970), 508-510.

Parker, A.A. "The Humour of Spanish Proverbs." *The Wisdom of Many. Essays on the Proverb.* Eds. Mieder,W. and Dundes A. New York: Garland Publishing, 1981. 257-74.

Pérez de Herrera, Cristóbal. *Proverbios morales.* Madrid, 1618.

ed. Plaza de Amo, F. *Diccionario Manual de Aforismos, Proverbios y Refranes.* Madrid, 1991.

Raymond, Joseph. "Using Proverbs in the Spanish Class." *Hispania,* 32 (1949), 215-221.

_____ *Attitudes and Cultural Patterns in Spanish Proverbs.* Diss. Columbia University, 1951.

_____ "Mexican Proverbs." *Western Folklore,* 12 (1953) 249-256.

Sánchez de la Ballesta, Alonso. *Diccionario de aforismos.* Madrid, 1587.

Sbarbi, José María. *Refranero general español.* Madrid, 1874-78.

Selig, Karl-Ludwig. "The Spanish Proverbs in Percyvall's «Spanish Grammar»." *Kentucky Romance Quarterly,* 17 (1970), 267-274.

_____ "The Spanish Proverbs in Hieronymus Megiserus." *Proverbium,* 16 (1971), 576.

_____ "An Important Seventeenth Century List of Spanish Proverbs." *Proverbium*, 22 (1973), 847-849.

Taylor, Archer. *The Proverb*. Cambridge, Mass.: Harvard University Press, 1931.

Vallejo, José Mariano. *Máximas militares y políticas*. Madrid, 1836.

Viada y Lluch, L.C. *Del amor al libro: aforismos rimados*. Barcelona, 1927.

_____ *Libro de oro de la vida: pensamientos, sentencias, máximas, proverbios*. Barcelona, 1905.

Viada y Vilaseca, Salvador. *Diccionario de la lengua española*. Apéndice III. Madrid, 1917.

Wilson, F.P. *The Oxford Dictionary of English Proverbs*. 3rd. ed. Oxford: OUP, 1970.

Young, Blamire. *The Proverbs of Goya. Being an Account of "Los Proverbios," Examined and Now for the First Time Explained*. New York: Houghton Mifflin, 1923.

English Key Word Index

NB   Index entries are arranged by *key word*, by which is meant the sequentially first noun most closely associated with the meaning of the proverb and/or having greater linguistic range or frequency. For proverbs without nouns, key words are verbs, adjectives or adverbs used on the basis of the same criteria. All numbers refer to the numbered Spanish proverb entries.

Spanish Interest Titles from Hippocrene . . .

Spanish-English/English-Spanish Concise Dictionary (Latin American)
by Ila Warner

The vast majority of Spanish-speaking people in America come from Latin American countries. This dictionary meets the needs of these Hispanic Americans and anyone wishing to communicate in the same Spanish most Americans speak. Includes 8,000 entries with pronunciation.

500 pages, 4 x 6
0-7818-0261-X, $11.95pb (0258)

Spanish-English/English-Spanish Dictionary of Computer Terms

This dictionary features over 5,700 English and Spanish computer terms. Common-sense pronunciation is included in both sections.

120 pages, 5 ½ x 8 ½
0-7818-0148-6, $16.95 (0036)

500 Spanish Words and Phrases
written and edited by
Carol Watson & Janet De Saulles

This book uses colorful cartoons to teach children basic Spanish phrases and vocabulary.

32 pages, 8 x 10 1/4, color illustrations
0-7818-0262-8, $8.95 (0017)

Spanish Verbs: Ser and Estar
by Juan & Susan Serrano
Finally, a volume to eliminate the confusion concerning the two Spanish verbs "to be."

220 pages, 5 ½ x 8 ½
0-7818-0024-2, $8.95pb (0292)

Spanish-English/English-Spanish Practical Dictionary
by Arthur S. Butterfield

338 pages, 5 ½ x 8 1/4
0-7818-0179-6, $9.95pb (0211)

Spanish Handy Dictionary

120 pages, 5 x 7 3/4
0-7818-0012-9, $8.95pb (0189)

Mastering Spanish
by Robert Clark

A useful tool for language learning, this method combines a full-size text with two audio cassettes allowing learners to hear proper pronunciation by native speakers as they study the book.

***Book:** 338 pages, 5 ½ x 8 ½*
0-87052-059-8, $11.95pb (0527)
2 Cassettes:
0-87052-067-9, $12.95 (0528)

Mastering Advanced Spanish

An advanced course of Spanish study utilizing the method of **Mastering Spanish**.

***Book:** 326 pages, 5 ½ x 8 ½*
0-7818-0081-1, $14.95pb (0413)
2 Cassettes:
0-7818-0089-7, $12.95pb (0426)

Spanish Literature from Hippocrene . . .

MISERICORDIA
Benito Perez Galdos
translated by Charles De Salis

Set among the poor of Madrid, this novel grapples
with the problem of goodness.
320 pgs, 1-873782-85-2
$16.95pb (0465)

TREASURY OF SPANISH LOVE
POEMS, QUOTATIONS AND
PROVERBS
in Spanish and English
edited and translated by
Juan and Susan Serrano

A bilingual gift collection of popular Spanish love
poems, spanning eight centuries. Works from De La
Vega, Garcia Lorca and Calderon offer insight into
the Spanish perspective on romance.
128 pages, 5 x 7
0-7818-0358-6, $11.95hc (0589)

Spanish Cooking with Hippocrene . . .

A SPANISH FAMILY COOKBOOK
FAVORITE FAMILY RECIPES
written by Juan and Susan Serrano

In this tantalizing guide to authentic Spanish cookery, Juan and Susan Serrano have culled over 250 of their favorite recipes from family menus and regional cuisine. The recipes are seasoned with commentaries on origin and regional variations, piquant observations on traditions and local customs and explanations of curious Spanish words and culinary proverbs. Features an entertaining and informative introduction to Spanish cuisine and has indexes in both Spanish and English.

Bilingual index, 247 pages, 6 x 9
0-7818-0193-1
$9.95pb (245)

Spanish Travel with Hippocrene. . .

LANGUAGE AND TRAVEL GUIDE
TO MEXICO
Ila Warner

This guide provides an excellent introduction to
Mexico for the traveler who wants to meet and
communicate with the people as well as sightsee. It
is also an ideal refresher course for those wishing to
brush up on their Spanish skills.

224 pages, maps, illustrations, index
5 1/2 x 8 1/2, 0-87052-622-7
$14.95pb (0503)

GUIDE TO
HISTORIC HISPANIC AMERICA
Oscar and Joy Jones

"Blends travel information with a Eurocentric view
of events... Chapters survey museums, historic sites,
and Spanish and Indian legends and lore."
— *Midwest Book Review*
"...this is an unusual guide that any serious traveler
to the Southwest United States would find
informative."
— *Library Journal*

300 pages, index, b/w photos, maps
5 1/2 x 8 1/2, 0-7818-0141-9
$14.95pb (0110)

Other Travel Guides
Available from Hippocrene . . .

All Guides: 5 x 8, $14.95pb

Language and Travel Guide to Australia
250 pages, illustrations, maps, index
0-7818-0166-4 (0086)

Language and Travel Guide to Britain
336 pages, maps, photos, index
0-7818-0290-3 (0119)

Language and Travel Guide to France
320 pages, 12 maps, index
0-7818-0080-3 (0386)

Language and Travel Guide to Indonesia
350 pages, photos, index
0-7818-0328-4 (0115)

Language and Travel Guide to Russia
293 pages, maps, b/w photos, index
0-7818-0047-1 (0321)

Language and Travel Guide to Ukraine
266 pages, maps, pictures, index
0-7818-0135-4 (0035)
$16.95 (new edition)

HIPPOCRENE BEGINNER'S SERIES

Do you know what it takes to make a phone call in Russia? To get through customs in Japan? How about inviting a Czech friend to dinner while visiting Prague? This new language instruction series shows how to handle typical, day-to-day situations by introducing the business person or traveler not only to the common vocabulary, but also to the history and customs.

The Beginner's Series consists of basic language instruction, which includes vocabulary, grammar, and common phrases and review questions; along with cultural insights, interesting historical background, the country's basic facts, and hints about everyday living.

Beginner's Bulgarian
Vacation travelers and students will find this volume a useful tool to understanding Bulgaria's language and culture. Dialogues include vocabulary and grammar rules likely to confront readers, and background on Bulgarian history is provided.
0-7818-0034-4 • $ 9.95

Beginner's Czech
The city of Prague has become a major tour destination for Americans who are now often choosing to stay. Here is a guide to the complex language spoken by the natives in an easy to learn format with a guide to phonetics. Also, important Czech history is outlined with cultural notes. This is another guide designed by Eurolingua.
0-7818-0231-8 • $9.95

Beginner's Esperanto
As a teacher of foreign languages for over 25 years, **Joseph Conroy** knows the need for people of different languages to communicate on a common ground. Though Esperanto has no parent country or land, it is developing an international society all its own. *Beginner's Esperanto* is an introduction to the basic grammar and vocabulary students will need to express their thoughts in the language.

At the end of each lesson, a set of readings gives the student further practice in Esperanto, a culture section presents information about the language and its speakers, a vocabulary lesson groups together all the words which occur in the text, and English translations for conversations allow students to check comprehension. As well, the author lists Esperanto contacts with various organizations throughout the world.
0-7818-0230-X • $14.95

Beginner's Hungarian

For the businessperson traveling to Budapest, the traveler searching for the perfect spa, or the Hungarian-American extending his or her roots, this guide by **Eurolingua** aids anyone searching for the words to express basic needs.
0-7818-0209-1 • $7.95

Beginner's Japanese

Author **Joanne Claypoole** runs a consulting business for Japanese people working in America. She has developed her Beginner's Guide for American businesspeople who work for or with Japanese companies in the U.S. or abroad.

Her book is designed to equip the learner with a solid foundation of Japanese conversation. Also included in the text are introductions to Hiragana, Katakana, and Kanji, the three Japanese writing systems.
0-7818-0234-2 • $11.95

Beginner's Polish

Published in conjunction with Eurolingua, *Beginner's Polish* is an ideal introduction to the Polish language and culture. Vocabulary adn grammar instruction is combined with information on the history and politics of Poland.
0-7818-0299-7 • $ 9.95
0-7818-0330-6 • $12.95 (cassettes)

Beginner's Romanian

This is a guide designed by **Eurolingua**, the company established in 1990 to meet the growing demand for Eastern European language and cultural instruction. The institute is developing books for business and leisure travelers to all Eastern European countries. This Romanian learner's guide is a one-of-a-kind for those seeking instant communication in this newly independent country.
0-7818-0208-3 • $7.95

Beginner's Russian

Eurolingua authors **Nonna Karr** and **Ludmila Rodionova** ease English speakers in the Cyrillic alphabet, then introduce enough language and grammar to get a traveler or businessperson anywhere in the new Russian Republic. This book is a perfect stepping-stone to more complex language.
0-7818-0232-6 • $9.95

Beginner's Swahili

An introductory course emphasizing conversation and basic grammar. Student progress when they are comfortabe using new skills in conversation. Includes a glossary of Swahili terms for quick reference.
0-7818-0335-7 • $ 9.95 (200 pages)
0-7818-0336-5 • $12.95 (cassettes)

HIPPOCRENE HANDY DICTIONARIES

For the traveler of independent spirit and curious mind, this practical series will help you to communicate, not just to get by. Common phrases are conveniently listed through key words. Pronunciation follows each entry and a reference section reviews all major grammar points. *Handy Extras* are extra helpful—offering even more words and phrases for students and travelers.

ARABIC
$8.95 • 0-87052-960-9

CHINESE
$8.95 • 0-87052-050-4

CZECH EXTRA
$8.95 • 0-7818-0138-9

DUTCH
$8.95 • 0-87052-049-0

FRENCH
$8.95 • 0-7818-0010-2

GERMAN
$8.95 • 0-7818-0014-5

GREEK
$8.95 • 0-87052-961-7

HUNGARIAN EXTRA
$8.95 • 0-7818-0164-8

ITALIAN
$8.95 • 0-7818-0011-0

JAPANESE
$8.95 • 0-87052-962-5

KOREAN
$8.95 • 0-7818-0082-X

PORTUGUESE
$8.95 • 0-87052-053-9

RUSSIAN
$8.95 • 0-7818-0013-7

SERBO-CROATIAN
$8.95 • 0-87052-051-2

SLOVAK EXTRA
$12.95 • 0-7818-0101-X

SPANISH
$8.95 • 0-7818-0012-9

SWEDISH
$8.95 • 0-87052-054-7

THAI
$8.95 • 0-87052-963-3

TURKISH
$8.95 • 0-87052-982-X

(All prices subject to change.)

TO PURCHASE HIPPOCRENE BOOKS contact your local bookstore, or write to: HIPPOCRENE BOOKS, 171 Madison Avenue, New York, NY 10016. Please enclose check or money order, adding $5.00 shipping (UPS) for the first book and $.50 for each additional book.

Hippocrene introduces . . .

BILINGUAL LOVE POETRY

The newest additions to Hippocrene's bilingual series are filled with romantic imagery and philosophical musings. These beautiful collections provide a glimpse of each culture's unique approach to affairs of the heart and cover such subjects as eternal love, unrequited love, pain, and parting. Readings of the selections, performed by native speakers, are available on cassettes as an accompaniment to each volume (approximate running time: 2 hours)

Treasury of Finnish Love
Poems, Quotations and Proverbs
Borje Vahamaki, editor & translator
128 pages, 5 x 7 0-7818-0397-7
(118) $11.95 cloth

Treasury of French Love
Poems, Quotations, and Proverbs
Richard A. Branyon, editor &
translator
128 pages, 5 x 7 0-7818-0307-1
(344) $11.95 cloth
Audiobook:
0-7818-0259-4
(580) $12.95

Treasury of German Love
Poems, Quotations, and Proverbs
Almut Hille, editor
128 pages, 5 x 7 0-7818-0296-2
(180) $11.95 cloth
Audiobook:
0-7818-0360-8
(577) $12.95

Treasury of Italian Love
Poems, Quotations and Proverbs
Richard Branyon, editor & translator
128 pages, 5 x 7 0-7818-0352-7
(587) $11.95 cloth
Audiobook:
0-7818-366-7
(581) $12.95 cloth

Treasury of Jewish Love
Poems, Quotations, and Proverbs
David Gross, editor
128 pages, 5 x 7 0-7818-0308-X
(346) $11.95 cloth
Audiobook:
0-7818-0363-2
(579) $12.95

Treasury of Polish Love
Poems, Quotations, and Proverbs
Miroslaw Lipinski, editor &
translator
128 pages, 5 x 7 0-7818-0397-0
Audiobook:
0-7818-0361-6
(576) $12.95

Treasury of Roman Love
Poems, Quotations, and Proverbs
Richard A. Branyon, editor &
translator
128 pages, 5 x 7 0-7818-0309-8
(348) $11.95 cloth

Treasury of Spanish Love
Poems, Quotations, and Proverbs
Juan and Susan Serrano, editors
128 pages, 5 x 7 0-7818-0358-6
(589) $11.95 cloth
Audiobook:
0-7818-0365-9
(584) $12.95

Treasury of Russian Love
Poems, Quotations, and Proverbs
Victorya Andreyeva, editor
128 pages, 5 x 7 0-7818-0298-9
(591) $11.95 cloth
Audiobook:
0-7818-0364-0
(586) $12.95

(All prices subject to change.)

TO PURCHASE HIPPOCRENE BOOKS contact your local bookstore, or write to:
HIPPOCRENE BOOKS, 171 Madison Avenue, New York, NY 10016. Please enclose
check or money order, adding $5.00 shipping (UPS) for the first book and $.50 for
each additional book.

Self-Taught Audio Language Courses

Hippocrene Books is pleased to recommend Audio-Forum self-taught language courses. They match up very closely with the languages offered in Hippocrene dictionaries and offer a flexible, economical and thorough program of language learning.

Audio-Forum audio-cassette/book courses, recorded by native speakers, offer the convenience of a private tutor, enabling the learner to progress at his or her own pace. They are also ideal for brushing up on language skills that may not have been used in years. In as little as 25 minutes a day — even while driving, exercising, or doing something else — it's possible to develop a spoken fluency.

Spanish Self-Taught Language Courses

Programmatic Spanish, Vol. I 12 cassettes (17 hr.), 464-p. text, manual, $185. Order #HS101. *Workbook for Spanish, Vol. I,* 128-p., $7.95. Order #HS990.

Programmatic Spanish, Vol. II 8 cassettes (12 hr.), 614-p. text, manual, $165. Order #HS121. *Workbook for Spanish, Vol. II,* 201-p., $14.95. Order #HS995.

Basic Spanish Advanced Level Part A, Units 31-45 12 cassettes (13 hr.), 614-p. text, $185. Order #HS153.

Basic Spanish Advanced Level Part B, Units 46-55 12 cassettes (12½ hr.), 472-p. text, $185. Order #HS170.

Medical Spanish (Beginning Course) 12 cassettes (11½ hr.), 256-p. text, 29-p. Listener's Guide, $195. Order #HMS20.

Business Spanish (Intermediate Course) 6 cassettes (6 hr.). 162-p. text, $185. Order #HS24300.

All Audio-Forum courses are fully guaranteed and may be returned within 30 days for a full refund if you're not completely satisfied.

You may order directly from Audio-Forum by calling toll-free 1-800-243-1234.

For a complete course description and catalog of 264 courses in 91 languages, contact Audio-Forum, Dept. SE5, 96 Broad St., Guilford, CT 06437. Toll-free phone 1-800-243-1234. Fax 203-453-9774.